TAHARAS AM YISROEL

PART I

הלכות נדה

A Practical Guide to the Laws of
Taharas Hamishpochoh

❧❧

PART II

★ *The Jewish Marriage*
★ *Sholom Bayis*

❧❧

Rabbi Shaul Wagschal

Jerusalem
2002/5762

By the same author:

Series of books on Practical Halochoh:	Series of books on Jewish Thought and Mussar:
Kashrus	With all your Heart (בטחון)
Taharas Hamishpocho, The Jewish Marriage & Sholom Bayis	Derech Eretz
	Towards Emunoh
	Guide to Teshuva
Care of Children on Shabbos, the Halachik problems	Successful Chinuch
	Why I married a Ben Torah
Childbirth on Shabbos	The Pleasant Ways of the Jewish Daughter
Laws for the Mourner and Comfort	
Guide to the Basics of Money Matters	
Laws of Interest (Ribis)	
What do you know about Money Matters	
More about Money Matters	
Laws of Yom Tov and Chol Hamoed	

Fourth Edition 2002/5762
Copyright © 1979, 1983, 1994, 1997

Hardcover edition: ISBN 0-87306-333-3
Paperback edition: ISBN 0-87306-334-1

Rabbi Shaul Wagschal
1341 47th Street
Brooklyn NY 11219 U.S.A.
718-851-4070

Distributed by

THE JUDAICA PRESS, INC
123 Ditmas Ave.
Brooklyn, NY 11218
718-972-6200   800-972-6201
info@judaicapress.com
www.judaicapress.com

Distributed in Europe by

Lehmanns
Unit E, Viking Industrial Park
Rolling Mill Road, Jarrow
Tyne and Wear, NE32 3DP England
+44 (0) 430 0333   Fax: 430 0555
info@lehmanns.co.uk

Printed in Israel

CONTENTS

Approbations (הסכמות) xi
Foreword xiv
A Plan of Study xvii
Glossary xx

PART I

CHAPTER ONE

Observance of *Ta'haras Ha'mishpochoh* - **A Marvel!** 1

CHAPTER TWO

Kedushas Am Yisroel 4

CHAPTER THREE

The Law of *Niddoh* 6
    A Mutual Responsibility 8

CHAPTER FOUR

First Step towards *Ta'haroh* (הפסק טהרה) 9
    Examination on the Fifth Day 9
    The Time of Examination 10
    On *Erev Shabbos* 11
    Preparing for Examination 11
    On *Shabbos, Yom Tov, Yom Kippur, Tish'oh B'Av*
    & During a *Shiv'oh* 12
    The Examination Cloth 13
    The Method of Examination 13
    Clean and Doubtful Results 14
    Unclean Result 15
    Additional Examination (מוך דחוק) 16

CHAPTER FIVE

The second step towards *Ta'haroh* (שבעה נקיים) **18**

    The Seven Clean Days 18
    Twice Daily Examinations 18
    Doubtful Examination 19
    Unsuccessful Examinations 20
    Omission of Examinations 20
    Asking a *Sha'aloh* 20

CHAPTER SIX

Preparing for Immersion **22**

    On the Day of *T'viloh* 23
    The Preparations 24
    Hair 24
    Nose, Ears & Eyes, Face, Mouth 25
    Fingers & Toes 26
    The Body 27
    Intervening Substances 28
    Plaster & Wounds 28
    Time of going to the *Mikveh* 29

CHAPTER SEVEN

***T'viloh* - the final step towards *Ta'haroh* (הטבילה)** **31**

    Check-up before *T'viloh* and *T'viloh* 32
    Posture during *T'viloh* 34
    Supervision 35
    Doubtful *T'viloh* 35
    T'viloh - A Private Matter 36
    On Coming Home 36

SUMMARY: FROM FIRST EXAMINATION TO IMMERSION

    (Chapters Four to Seven) 37

CHAPTER EIGHT

T'viloh* on *Shabbos* or *Yom Tov **42**

    When to Light the Candles 43
    Preparations not Finished before *Shabbos* 44
    Unlit *Mikveh* on *Shabbos* 45

CHAPTER NINE

T'viloh after *Shabbos*, on *Yom Tov*, *Tish'oh B'Av*
or *Yom Kippur* 47

CHAPTER TEN

***T'viloh* on Time** 50

    T'viloh after Childbirth 51

CHAPTER ELEVEN

How a woman becomes *Niddoh* 52

    Compulsory Investigation 53
    Niddoh not due to a Period 54
    Colours of Discharge 54
    Internal Wounds 55
    Bleeding after Marital Relations (רואה מחמת תשמיש) 55

CHAPTER TWELVE

Menstruation Dates (פרישה סמוך לווסת) 56

    When to Separate 57
    Examination on Menstruation Dates 58
    After Menstruation Dates 58

CHAPTER THIRTEEN

Calculating Menstruation Dates 59

    Period Preceded by Symptoms 61
    Fluctuation within Three Days 62
    Fresh Bleeding after Short Interval 62
    The Menopause 63

CHAPTER FOURTEEN

"Spotting" (כתמים) 64

    Size of Stain 65
    Spots on Coloured Material 65
    When to Ask a *Sha'aloh* 66

CHAPTER FIFTEEN

Conduct during Unclean Days (הרחקות בימי נדתה) 68

    Touching and Passing of Objects 68
    Sharing a Seat 68
    Eating Together 69

Serving Food 71
Personal Attention:
   Making the bed 72
   Preparing water for washing 72
Attention during Illness 72
Travelling Together 74
Conversation etc. 74

CHAPTER SIXTEEN

Laws for a Bride 76
Fixing the Wedding 76
Preparing for the Wedding 77

CHAPTER SEVENTEEN

After the Wedding 78
A Bride who is *Niddoh* 78
The First Night 78
The First *Ta'haroh* Procedure 79
The First *T'viloh* Night after Marriage 80
Examination before and after Marital Relationships 81

CHAPTER EIGHTEEN

Pregnancy and Childbirth 82
A Woman in Labour 83
After Childbirth 83
After a Miscarriage 83
First Two Years after Childbirth 83

CHAPTER NINETEEN

The Irregular Period (וסת שאינו קבוע) 85
The Cycles:
   The Lunar Cycle (וסת החודש) 86
   The Same-Interval Cycle (וסת הפלגה) 86
   The Thirty-Days Cycle (עונה בינונית) 87
   Physical-Symptoms Cycle (וסת הגוף) 89

CHAPTER TWENTY

The Regular Period (וסת קבוע) 91
Changing from Irregular to Regular Period 92
Recognizing a Regular Period 92

Menstruation Dates for the Regular Period (יום ווסת) 94
Missing a Period 94
Changing from Regular to Irregular or to Another
Regular Period 95
Differences between Regular and Irregular Period 96

CHAPTER TWENTY ONE

More About *Kedushoh* 97

CHAPTER TWENTY TWO

Extracts of an Address to Women by *Rabbenu Yonah* 99

תפלה לבנים ולהצלחתם .... ב - ג

HEBREW FOOTNOTES

To Chapters Two, Three and Twenty-One
(to be read from right to left) .... ד - ה

PART II

CHAPTER ONE

Marriage Obligations 111
The husband's obligations 111
The wife's obligations 112
Money brought into the marriage 113
Presents given to a wife by other parties 113
Management of money 113
Kibbud av vo'aim 114

CHAPTER TWO

The Jewish Marriage 115
Introduction 115
Kedusho 116
Tznius 117
Dinim of *tznius* 118
Motivation and attitude 119

CHAPTER THREE

The Torah View on Family Planning 124

Contraception 124
Sterilization 125
Abortion 125

CHAPTER FOUR

The Concept of *Tznius* 127

What is *tznius* 127
Tznius in practical manifestations 128
Tznius—not a Jewish invention 129
Tznius in the home 130

CHAPTER FIVE

Tznius* in *Halocho 131

Dress 131
Swimming 132
Exercising in front of men 133
Hair covering 133
Not completely dressed 134
Singing 134

CHAPTER SIX

Married people vis-a-vis other men or women 135

A fiance and his bride 136
Medical attention 136

CHAPTER SEVEN

Kissing Relatives 137

Introduction to the laws of kissing relatives 137
Blood relations and non-blood relations 137
Stages of a girl's maturity 138
A boy's age of maturity 138
Kissing relatives—when allowed and when not 138

CHAPTER EIGHT

Adopted and Step-children 139

Status 139

Guidance to Sholom Bayis

CHAPTER NINE

Looking forward to Marriage **145**

    The wife of a *talmid chochom* 146

CHAPTER TEN

The aspirations of young singles before marriage **148**

    A girl's aspirations 148

    The young man's hopes 149

CHAPTER ELEVEN

Understanding one another **150**

    Differences between men and women 151

    Modesty 157

CHAPTER TWELVE

Ways to achieve harmony in marriage **160**

    Marital harmony 161

    The wife's role 161

    The husband's role 162

    Conversation as a means to achieving harmony 162

CHAPTER THIRTEEN

The Husband — the captain of the household **165**

    The husband's contribution 165

    Some guidelines for making decisions 166

    Who to seek advice from 167

    How to ask for advice 168

CHAPTER FOURTEEN

A Woman of Valour **169**

CHAPTER FIFTEEN

Basic Necessities **171**

    How do we define necessities 171

    Duties set out in the *kesubo* 172

CHAPTER SIXTEEN

Her home is her castle **173**

Is it advisable for a woman to go out to work? 173

CHAPTER SEVENTEEN

The woman's share in *Avodas Hashem* 176

CHAPTER EIGHTEEN

Give and Take 178

Kindness 179

CHAPTER NINETEEN

Who takes priority — her husband or her children.................... 181

CONCLUSION 184

מקורות והערות—Hᴇʙʀᴇᴡ Fᴏᴏᴛɴᴏᴛᴇs 200

הסכמת הרה"ג ר' יצחק יעקב וייס זצ"ל
גאב"ד לכל מקהלות האשכנזים עיה"ק ירושלים תובב"א

הנה כבר איתמחי גברא יקירא ה"ה הרה"ג חו"ב וכו' כש"ת מוה"ר
שאול וגשאל שליט"א מגייטסהעד יצ"ו בחיבוריו לזכות הרבים בהעלות
על שולחן העם בלשון המובן להם קובצים עיקרי דינים השכיחים במידי
דאית רבותא לינוקא, ולהורות את הדרך אשר ילכו בה דיני שבת ויום טוב
ואיסור והיתר וכבר נתפשטו בכמה מהדורות בין הבע"ב היראים להציל
רבים ממכשולות שנכשלו בחסרון ידיעה, וזכות הרבים בידו.

ועכשיו רחש לבו עוד דבר טוב לעשות בעמו לבאר הדינים הנחוצים
לחיי המשפחה בישראל בקדושה ובטהרה, היינו דיני אישות איסור מניעת
הריון והלכות צניעות ודיני יחוד והלכות נדה וכיב"ז, דמי שלא למד ולא
שנה וחזר על ההלכות מדי יום ביומו אי אפשר שלא יכשל בהם ח"ו.

והרה"ג הנ"ל יגע ושנה ויגיעתו עמדה לו לסדר סידורי הלכות
בקיצור בעניינים הנזכרים אשר שאב מבאר מים חיים של הפוסקים אשר
מפיהם אנו חיים ואת מקורם הערה בציוני המקורות אשר יאמר עם
הספר, ומובטחני שתביא תועלת רב לכל המעיינים בספרו ויתגלגל זכות
על ידי זכאי ואמינא לפעלא טבא יישר ויזכה לראות פרי טוב בעמלו ונזכה
לגאולה וישועה קרובה לבוא בביאת משיח צדקינו בב"יא

בעה"ח לכבוד התורה והמצוה עש"יק לסדר זאת חקת התורה
תשל"יה לפ"יק

יצחק יעקב וייס גאב"ד פעה"ק ירושת"ו

הסכמת הרה״ג ר׳ שמואל הלוי ואזנר שליט״א

אב״ד ור״מ זכרון-מאיר בני-ברק

יום כ״ב סיון תשל״ה לפ״ק

הנה כבוד שו״ב ההי״ג בנש״ק מזכה את הרבים מוהר״ר שאול וואגשאל שליט״א מעיר גייטסהעד דאנגליא הראה לפני קונטרס ״טהרת עם ישראלי׳ כולל בתוכו ח״א הלכות נחוצות למעשה בענין התרחקות מעריות וקדושת ישראל בכלל, וח״ב קצור דיני טבילה ונדה שניהם בשפה האנגלית ואת מקור ההלכות הערה בטוטו״ד בלה״ק בטעם זקנים, כולם יסודם בהררי קודש פוסקים המקובלים על רבותינו זי״ע. וכבר איתמחי גברא גבר בגוברין שליט״א בחיבוריו כיו״ב על הלכות כשרות וכו׳ ג״כ בשפה הנ״ל וזכה שנתקבל ונתפשט בין ההמונים וכבר נדפס ג״פ לזכות הרבים ולקרב רחוקים לדיני וקדושת ישראל.

ע״כ גם ידי תכון עמו כי ידעתי כוונתו לשם שמים ע״כ יהי׳ גם מעשיו חיים וקיימים.

המצפה לרחמי ה׳ מרובים

שמואל הלוי ואזנר

הסכמת הרה"ג ר' שלמה זלמן אויערבאך שליט"א

הרב שלמה זלמן אויערבאך
פעיה"ק **ירושלים** תובב"א

ב"ה, יום .... ל.......... תש....

הובא לפני עלים להרה"ג רב .... נ"י ....
ועם .. הנה הרבה זכות וולגבולין שלהם, ואף ....
נפשו הרבה זכרונות מסוף .... מה .... הכרעות
ונראה .... כי ...... ראוי ....
תעי ....
עלים ..... ולפ..... ..... על כל דיעות ......
.... להרבות ....
.... לאחדות ....
.... לאויריא ......
.... תעלה ....
.... ולצאת דבר רבים.

שלמה זלמן אויערבאך

FOREWORD TO
THE FOURTH EDITION AND PART TWO

In this edition we have joined Part One and Two of Taharas and Kedushas Am Yisroel into one book.

Part Two deals with matters which are essential for a couple who want to make a success of their mariage in the spirit of Torah and *halacha*.

The preparation of a *choson* and *kallo* for marriage would be incomplete without reading the relevant chapters near the time of their marriage.

A special feature is the section on Sholom Bayis. The author has used an original approach and it is hoped that it will assist young people in building a בית נאמן בישראל.

Iyar 5762   S. W.

FOREWORD TO FIRST EDITION

Taharas Am Yisroel is designed both to prepare a *choson* and a *kalloh* for marriage and to act as a guide to married couples in matters of *ta'haras ha'mishpochoh*.

The main concern has been to present the subject in a concise and lucid manner, without sacrificing detail. The author has had to bear in mind also, the delicate nature of the subject and the sensitive feelings of the reader. The author has attempted, therefore, to set the reader in a frame of mind which will lead him to observe the laws with understanding and joy.

The Manuscript. The Manuscript was read by ladies with many years of experience in instructing *kallos*. Their invaluable suggestions resulted in the complete rewriting of some sections.

Appreciations. I am indebted to Rabbi A Katz (Gateshead) for reading the manuscript with meticulous care and for his numerous amendments. I further wish to express my thanks to Rabbi Shimon Beton *zatzal*, Head of the *Beth Din* and *Kollel* of Marseilles (France) for writing a part of the footnotes; also to all who offered constructive advice and to the publishers for their skill in producing the book in its present form.

ויהי רצון שלא אכשל בדבר הלכה ולא יבא שום מכשול על ידי

חנוכה תשל״ו   Shaul Wagschal

FOREWORD TO SECOND EDITION

I wish to thank all those who offered valuable suggestions for improvements to the book.

I am grateful especially to Rabbi Moshe Santhouse of Manchester and above all to Rabbi A L Louis of Kolel Mir, Jerusalem (now *Dayan* in Amsterdam), and his wife who greatly assisted in revising the text.

I wish to take this opportunity to perpetuate the name of Mrs. Martha Miriam Hubert ע״ה, the late wife of Mr. Arthur Hubert ז״ל.

Mrs. Hubert who was an aristocratic lady with a warm Jewish heart, took a special interest in endearing *Taharas Ha'mishpochoh* to the younger generation. She felt so strongly about it, that she herself published an interesting and attractive pamphlet on this subject.

Mrs. Hubert will be remembered, also, for assisting her husband in his world-wide support of Jewish Day Schools, Yeshivos, Kolelim, Seminaries and other Torah-true causes, and particularly in his work for the Gateshead Foundation for Torah ת.נ.צ.ב.ה.

טבת תשמ״ב   S .W.

A Plan Of Study

For the Kalloh and a married woman who has decided to keep *ta'haras ha'mishpochoh* for the first time.

You are embarking on the study of an unfamiliar subject and you will be introduced to new concepts. If you read the book on your own and come across difficulties, do not hesitate to ask a relative or a friend for help. Many people find this subject confusing, at first. Your aim must be to *master the basic laws* i.e. those laws which *you* will have to put into practice before and after the marriage. Therefore, do not read too much at one time. Make sure that you understand each step before you move on to the next.

Here is a suggested study programme:-

a) Read Chapters One, Two and Three. This will show you *how* to approach the subject and what it is all about.

b) Study Chapters Four to Seven and then Chapter Ten. You will need to put these laws into practice even *before* your marriage. Glance at the *first* paragraph of Chapter Sixteen at the first opportunity, as this is important for fixing the date of your Wedding.

Make use of the GLOSSARY to become familiar with the Hebrew terms.

c) After learning how to prepare for marriage (a process which will need to be practiced *every* time a woman becomes *niddoh)*, you will need to know also the laws which apply during marriage. These are set out in the following chapters:

1)   Chapter Eleven - How a woman becomes a *niddoh*.

2)   Chapter Fourteen - "Spotting" and when to ask a *Sha'aloh*.

3)   Chapter Twelve - "Menstruation Dates".

4)   Chapter Fifteen - Conduct during the *niddoh* period.

d)   You may now attempt to learn Chapter Thirteen. If after reading it two or three times, you still find it difficult - do not panic. 'You are not alone' - many people have this problem. The usual solution is to work out the *calculations* together with your husband.

e)   Shortly before your wedding read Part I Chapters Sixteen and Seventeen and Part II Chapter Two to Five.

f)   Chapters Eight and Nine deal with *t'viloh* on or after *Shabbos* or *Yom Tov*. This is not an everyday occurrence and there is no need to learn it at this stage. This applies also to Chapter Eighteen. It is not essential for women to master Chapters Nineteen and Twenty.

Note: A well-tried idea is to revise the *dinim* early in marriage with your husband.

For the Choson and married man

This book covers all the basic laws of *ta'haras ha'mishpochoh* i.e. those that apply to a woman only and those that apply equally to husband and wife. Chapters Four to Ten deal with the *dinim* which apply to the wife. The rest applies equally to husband and wife. It is useful for the husband to know, also, the laws pertaining to his wife, as this will enable him to understand *her* problems and to give her advice and guidance.

Here is a suggested programme:-

1) Chapters One, Two and Three - An introduction to the subject.

2) Chapter Eleven - How a woman becomes a *niddoh*.

3) Chapters Twelve and Thirteen - "Menstruation Dates".

4) Chapter Fourteen - "Spotting".

5) Chapter Fifteen - Conduct during the *niddoh* period.

6) Chapter Thirteen - Calculating "Menstruation Dates". [Chapters Nineteen and Twenty should preferably be learned before the Wedding.]

7) Chapter Ten - *T'viloh* on time.

8) Near the time of the Wedding read Part I Chapters Sixteen, Seventeen and Chapter Twenty One and Part II Chapter Two to Five.

General

It is usual to review the *dinim* from time to time, especially after the birth of a child. It is also important for the sake of clarity to discuss the *dinim* with one's wife.

The extracts of ״אמירה לבית יעקב״ (page 99) will form a good basis for discussions related to the Jewish marriage and חינוך.

GLOSSARY

B'DIKOH
Internal examination to check for the presence of blood.

B'ROCHOH
Blessing.

CHOL HA'MOED
The intermediate days of Passover and Tabernacles.

CHOMETZ
Leaven.

CHOSON
Bridegroom.

DIN (pl. DINIM)
Jewish Law or a Jewish law.

EREV PESSACH
Eve of Passover.

HEF'SEK TA'HAROH
Preliminary examination which establishes that bleeding has stopped.

HE'TER
Permission in accordance with Jewish law.

KALLOH
Bride.

KEDUSHOH
Holiness

MA'ARIV
Evening Service.

MIKVEH
Gathering of water in a structure conforming to the laws of ritual immersion; the complex of rooms

MOTZEI	The night after ....
MUK'TZEH	An object one is forbidden to move on *Shabbos* or *Yom Tov*.
NIDDOH	State of ritual impurity caused by menstruation or other bleeding from the womb.
POSEK	Rabbinical authority.
RAV	Rabbi having *s'michoh*.
RIBONO SHEL O'LOM	Master of the Universe.
SHAMOSH	Personal attendant of a Rabbi.
SHIV'OH	The seven days of mourning.
SHKI'OH	Sunset.
SMI'CHOH	Authorisation to make rabbinical decisions.
TA'HARAS HA'MISHPOCHOH	Purity in Jewish family life.
TA'HOR or TA'HAROH	State of purity attained after immersion in a *mikveh*.
TOVEL	To immerse.
TO'MEH	Ritually unclean.
TZNI'US	Chastity.

PART I

Taharas Hamishpocho

CHAPTER ONE

OBSERVANCE OF TA'HARAS HA'MISHPOCHOH

— A MARVEL

There is a well known story of the famous Reb Levi Yitzchok of Berdichev. Once on *Erev Pessach* afternoon, he sent his *shamosh* to buy beer from a Jewish house in Berdichev. The *shamosh* was puzzled. Beer is *chometz*! How can he, the *shamosh* of Reb Levi Yitzchok, come to a Jew on *Erev Pessach* with such a request? But the Rebbe's orders must be obeyed. He knocked on the door of the first Jewish house and delivered the Rebbe's message. The reply was sharp and to the point: "There must be something wrong with you. We keep no beer on *Pessach*!" The *shamosh* went from house to house, but everywhere the answer was the same.

He returned to the Rebbe empty-handed.

"Now try to buy me some tobacco; lots of it, as much as you can carry," said the Rebbe.

This was another puzzle. Why does the Rebbe need so much tobacco on *Erev Pessach*? And, besides, will anyone dare to sell tobacco? (The sale of tobacco was strictly controlled in those days and could be sold only by license.) But orders are orders, so without more ado he made his second round of Berdichev. It was not long before the *shamosh* returned loaded with skillfully camouflaged tobacco.

The Rebbe glanced at the tobacco and smiled with satisfaction. He raised his eyes to heaven and said:

"*Ribono shel O'lom*! What a wonderful nation are your *Am Yisroel*! Here rules the mighty and strong Tzar! He has policemen. He has judges and courts, officers and prisons. Yet, when he decrees that private sale of tobacco is a crime, does anyone obey? Does anyone care? But *your* people! They have no soldiers and no policemen, no officers and no prisons. But, because You said in Your holy Torah: "Keep no *chometz* on *Pessach*!" no Jew has *chometz*, no Jew has beer. My *shamosh* has been round the whole Berdichev. Did he find any *chometz*? Did he find any beer? Is there any other nation like *Am Yisroel*?" מי כעמך ישראל!

This is the uniqueness of the Jewish people. There is no human control or supervision and yet, *Torah* laws are meticuously observed. This quality is displayed, par excellence, in the sphere of *ta'haras ha'mishpochoh* where there is complete trust in the integrity of the Jewish woman.

She is honest to herself, honest to her husband and honest to *Hashem*.

The Guardian of the Sanctity of the Jewish Nation

By entering wedlock the Jewish daughter becomes the guardian of the sanctity of the Jewish nation in general and of *her* family in particular. This noble task has been carried out by myriads of women throughout the ages with conscientiousness and chastity and with awareness of their great responsibility.

CHAPTER TWO

KEDUSHAS AM YISROEL

Kedushoh means separation[א][1] It also means holiness.[ב]
According to the Torah a person who restrains himself from
earthly desires, even if only temporarily, is considered as being
holy.[ג]

Man was created with the power of reproduction. *Hashem*
designed that this should be used only in marriage.[ז] Yet, from
the time of puberty a youth already possesses this faculty, with
the accompanying emotions. Those who follow the path of the
Torah strive to keep their thoughts and emotions under control,
even during the years of adolescence and beyond, in spite of the
many difficulties involved.[ח] This is *kedushoh*!

Kedushoh exists also after marriage.[ט]

One of the purposes of marriage is that each partner shields
the other from sin.[י] The first year of marriage the *shonoh*

---

1. See Hebrew notes at end of book.

ri'shonoh, was instituted by the Torah to lay the foundation for this [n]. The *Chinuch* puts it like this: In their first year husband and wife should become so acclimatised to the nature of the other that after that year they will reject automatically all feelings towards someone outside their marriage.[v]

Kedushoh in marriage, especially for men, means that marriage should not become a vehicle for following one's impulses by letting go, even though in a permitted way (see Part II Chapter Two).[r] There is also a danger that indulgence could be white-washed by the pretext that it is done for the sake of *chesed* or that through that the marriage will grow.

Instead, marriage should be utilised as an instrument for fostering moral refinement.[n"]

This Chapter touches on *kedushoh* in marriage only in general terms. More guidance will be given in Part II Chapter Two pages 115-116.

The reader must be aware that *kedushoh* is a virtue for which one should strive whereas the *Niddoh Law*, which is the main subject of this book is mandatory and no detail of it must be taken lightly.

CHAPTER THREE

THE LAW OF
NIDDOH

The Torah states: ואל אשה בנדת טומאתה לא תקרב וכו'
(ויקרא פרק י"ח פ' י"ט) "You shall not come near to a woman
during the time of her menstrual[1] *niddoh* impurity".

This law implies that from the onset of the period or *any*
show of blood originating from the womb even during pregnancy
or after the menopause) until after immersion in a *mikveh* the
relationship between husband and wife is to be limited to
friendship as distinct from physical intimacy. Immersion must be
preceded by a period of preparation which is the subject of the

---

1. A *niddoh* is considered *to'meh* (i.e. ritually impure) also in relation to
other *ta'haroh* laws, e.g. she may not enter the area encircled by the outer
walls of the *Beth Ha'mikdosh* (i.e. the *har ha'bayis*). She may not eat holy
food (*tru'moh* and *ko'desh*) and everything she touches becomes likewise
to'meh. This latter law has no practical application nowadays, but the law of
not entering the *har ha'bayis*, *is* applicable nowadays to women and men
alike.

following chapters. The total time of this restriction usually lasts from twelve to fifteen days.

One need not fear that these periodic times are a strain on the marriage. The truth is that times of temporary restraint have a stabilizing influence on the marriage. They introduce an element of continuous freshness which revitalizes and strengthens the bond between husband and wife. This is not the purpose of the law, but it is one beneficial side effect.

It will be comforting to know in advance, that in spite of husband and wife being in such close proximity, it does not require a great amount of self-control to keep their distance, as long as they are aware of the severity of this command.

This *niddoh-law* is a *chok*, i.e. the limits of human perception make it impossible to discover the true reason for this G-d-given law. Yet, the Torah attaches so much importance to it, that non-conformity with the law attracts a punishment similar to that of idolatry and adultery.[ב'] In common with these two (and with shedding of human blood), a Jew is obliged to give up his life rather than transgressing the law of *niddoh*.[ג'] This requirement of literal *mesiras nefesh* applies mainly to men and not to women because they are involved only in a passive capacity.[ד'] The impurity of *niddoh* can be transferred also to a man, as stated explicitly in the Torah (Vayikroh 11,24). It is lamentable that there are so many who do not give serious thought to this subject. Do they realise that by one ill-timed act they pull themselves down into the abyss of impurity? (unless they later raise themselves up through *teshuvoh*).

On the other hand, how fortunate are those who live a life of *taharoh* and who see in self-restraint and in the extra effort (i.e. the preparation for and the actual *teviloh*) a fulfillment rather than a burden.

All girls prior to marriage and all unmarried women are nowadays in a state of *niddoh*, since only married women prepare for immersion. It is worth noting that immersion without the *correct* discipline of the preparations is of *very little* value. A woman remains *niddoh* indefinitely, even beyond the menopause, unless immersion and the proper preparation for it would take place.

OBSERVING THE LAW

A mutual responsibility

The practical observance of the *ta'haroh* laws is mainly a matter for the wife, nevertheless the co-operation of the husband is required in a number of areas. It is vital, therefore, to establish a good relationship from the start so that problems raised by one can be viewed by the other with sympathy and understanding. An atmosphere of trust and mutual respect should prevail at all times. Although discussion of personal matters should be conducted with *tzni'us* clarity should not be sacrificed.

Coping with difficulties

It is common to have initial difficulties when attempting to put the laws into practice. Some find the calculations complicated. Others are not sure of the timing of the examinations or find it hard to grasp the practical side. All doubts *must* be clarified. One must neither imagine nor guess nor take a chance. One must become absolutely clear about every aspect of the laws.

CHAPTER FOUR

FIRST STEP TOWARDS TA'HAROH

הפסק טהרה

Examination On or After the Fifth Day (*Hef'sek Ta'haroh*)

The purpose of this examination is to establish whether bleeding or staining has completely stopped. The examination (*b'dikoh*) may take place on the fifth day after onset of the period *but not before*[1], even if bleeding has stopped earlier. If one is still bleeding or staining on the fifth day the examination is postponed for a day or two, or until there is no more staining.

The Fifth Day

One counts the day the period began as the first of the five days. This applies regardless of whether the bleeding started

1. An exception is made in the case of a *Kalloh* (See Page 77).

during the day or the previous night (as the Jewish day starts at nightfall, just as *Shabbos* starts on Friday evening). Briefly: Call the day the period began "day one" and count another four days.

Formula: Count the day on which the period began plus four days.

1st day	*5th day*
Sunday	Thursday afternoon
Monday	Friday afternoon
Tuesday	Shabbos afternoon
Wednesday	Sunday afternoon
Thursday	Monday afternoon
Friday	Tuesday afternoon
Shabbos	Wednesday afternoon

Note: If bleeding began in the evening after sunset a *sha'aloh* is required as to how to calculate the five days.

TIME OF EXAMINATION

Before Sunset

The examination (*b'dikoh*) takes place *on* the fifth day shortly[2] before[3] sunset (*shki'oh*). Sunset: The time of sunset fluctuates between 20 minutes (in Israel) and one hour or more (in other parts of the world) before "night" depending also on the season of the year. If the time of sunset is not known one can be guided by the Jewish calendar which has the times of the commencement of *Shabbos*. One looks up the time of the

---

2. Preferably within half an hour of sunset.
3. i.e. when the sun is still visible on the horizon.

commencement of *Shabbos* of the previous[4] and the following week and takes the *earlier* time. The resulting time will be at least 10 minutes before sunset.

Example: Previous *Shabbos* commenced at 6.14 p.m.; the next *Shabbos* commences 6.00 p.m. Therefore examination may take place up to approximately 6.00 p.m.

Note: *Hef'sek ta'haroh* made after sunset is normally not valid. If it took place a *few* minutes after sunset a *sha'aloh* should be asked. (This does not apply in Eretz Yisroel where sunset *is* the limit.)

Before Ma'ariv

In the summer in a place where all the local synagogues recite *ma'ariv* well before nightfall the *b'dikoh* should preferably be made beforehand. If she was delayed she may make it until sunset. Furthermore, *she herself* should not recite *ma'ariv* before the *b'dikoh*.

On Erev Shabbos

On the eve of *Shabbos* and *Yom Tov* the *b'dikoh* should be made before lighting the candles. If *she* was delayed, or forgot, the examination can still be made until sunset.

PREPARING FOR THE EXAMINATION

Washing

She first takes a bath or washes herself thoroughly with warm water to remove all traces of blood. This is usually done about half an hour before sunset, or earlier if she prefers.

---

4. Note: after the 21st of June, the following *Shabbos* shows the earlier time and after the 21st of December, the previous *Shabbos* has the earlier time.

It is suggested that a preliminary test is made to see:

a) if the actual bleeding has ceased;

b) if all traces of blood have been removed.

Note: People with a sensitive skin or who experience difficulties with examinations should attempt the *proper* examination immediately after the washing.

If the test shows no evidence of fresh bleeding but only faint red marks she should wash again and repeat the test. If after further washing red marks are again noticed, she must assume that the bleeding has not entirely ceased and a further attempt should be made the following day.

If the cloth is clean she is in a position to perform the proper internal examination.

On Shabbos and *Yom Tov*

Although she may not have a bath it is permitted to wash with cold or warm water provided she does not use solid soap, a cloth or a sponge. The examination cloth must be prepared before *Shabbos*.

On Yom Kippur or Tish'oh B'av or during a Shiv'oh[5]

Although normal washing is not permitted on these days, nevertheless washing the necessary area in preparation of the *Hef'sek Ta'haroh* examination is permitted (but not washing etc. in preparation for *t'viloh*).

---

5. The seven days of mourning.

THE EXAMINATION

The Examination Cloth

Examinations are made with a soft, white, perfectly clean absorbent[6] material[7] (usually a piece of old laundered cotton material). Tampons, paper, synthetic or any rough material e.g. new linen or starched cloth may not be used.

The size should be approximately 8 x 8 cm or *a little larger*[8]. Examination cloths should be kept in a clean place e.g. a large envelope.

Method of *B'dikoh* - הבדיקה

a) She waits a few minutes after the washing. Before the *b'dikoh* she examines the cloth on both sides to ensure that it is perfectly clean. She then wraps it around her forefinger[9] and makes a thorough yet gentle internal examination by inserting her finger with the cloth into the vagina *and* by pressing the cloth against all its sides. This is achieved by turning the finger slowly once in one direction and then in the other. The insertion should be as deep as her finger allows.[10] This is best achieved by raising one foot and resting it on a chair. A superficial examination is not valid. It is advisable to receive guidance from an experienced woman as to the manner of this *b'dikoh*.

Note: If, she has a ring or anything else inserted within the body for medical reasons, an urgent *sha'aloh* is required as

---

6. Many object to the use of cotton wool as some of its fibres may become detached and may not be available for inspection.
7. A closely woven material, as thin and fine as possible.
8. but not less than approximately 6 x 6 cm.
9. Under no circumstance should a woman use anything but her finger.
10. A *Kalloh* will usually not be able to insert her finger very deep.

to how this affects the *b'dikoh*.

b)   The cloth must then be carefully scrutinised to see whether it is perfectly clean and free from any substance. White or off-white, which is the colour of the natural mucus, is considered as *clean*. All other colours are subject to rabbinical decision. Even the smallest dot with a red shade renders the examination *unclean*.

Even if one has reason to believe that the red mark is due to a sore or wound it must be submitted to a *Rav* for his decision.

It is wrong to postpone the *b'dikoh* for another day in order to avoid asking a *sha'aloh* on the *b'dikoh* as this may cause a delay of the *t'viloh*.

c)   Inspection of the cloth should be done by daylight as colours cannot be identified easily by artificial light. If an inspection was made at night with a satisfactory result and the cloth is not available for re-inspection during the following day, she may rely on the original inspection. She should not inspect the cloth when the sun shines directly onto it nor in a place where there could be a reflection from a red material e.g. red curtains.

People suffering from myopia (i.e. short-sightedness) should take note that when they look very close small marks or dots can sometimes be detected only *without* spectacles.

Doubtful Results

If the cloth is not perfectly clean a *sha'aloh* is required.

If it is still before sunset she may attempt a further

examination which may turn out to be perfect.[11] If the result is still doubtful she should send *both* to a *Rav*.

In the meantime, although the *sha'aloh* is not yet resolved, she should continue with the normal routine so that in case it would be ruled to be *clean* a day will not have been lost unnecessarily. If the *Rav* ruled that the *b'dikoh* was not clean a fresh *hef'sek ta'haroh* will be required the following day.

Doubtful substances e.g. black, red or brown dots noticed on the cloth must not be removed. The cloth should be carefully folded inwards and put into a clean wrapper (not made from plastic) or envelope and a *Rav* must be consulted.

Unclean Result

If the *b'dikoh* was not satisfactory and it is still before sunset she may attempt further examinations.[12] If these are again unsatisfactory she postpones the examination until the following day.

If a woman has continuous difficulties in obtaining clean results rabbinical *and*, possibly, medical advice should be sought.

Clean Result - הפסק טהרה

If she is satisfied that the cloth is clean she can assume that the bleeding has ceased (i.e. *hefsek ta'haroh*) and prepare for the interim of the so called *seven clean days* - the second step of the *ta'haroh* process. Meanwhile, her *niddoh* status is as yet unchanged.

---

11. See note on Page 19.
12. Obviously this does not apply for a *b'dikoh* of the *seven days*. See Chapter 5.

Preparing for the Seven Clean Days - לבישת לבנים

She must wear fresh white underwear and use clean white bed linen during the *seven clean days*. If no fresh underwear is available, then she should examine what she has been wearing. If it is free from stains, it may be used, otherwise she will have to wash off the stains. The same applies to bed linen. Underwear should be changed before sunset, after the successful *hef'sek ta'haroh*.

Additional Examination - מוך דחוק

It is widely accepted that a further, longer-lasting *b'dikoh* is made to ascertain that there is no recurrence of bleeding at the end of the day.[13] In certain instances this extra *b'dikoh* is compulsory. She starts this second *b'dikoh* shortly before sunset by inserting a fresh cloth into the vagina without turning it round. There is no need to press the cloth against all sides of the vagina for this *b'dikoh*. She leaves it inserted until after nightfall. The cloth is inspected at night, placed in a clean place and re-inspected next morning by daylight. If it is *clean* she may start to count the *Seven Clean Days*.

If this *b'dikoh* was missed out she should ask a *sha'aloh*.

Note: This additional *b'dikoh* cannot replace the proper *hef'sek ta'haroh* examination.

If she has difficulties in making the additional *b'dikoh* or, if continuous *sha'alos* are caused on account of it, guidance should be sought from a *Rav* concerning the need of this additional *b'dikoh*.

---

13. A *Kalloh* who is still a true *bessuloh* (a virgin) does not need this second *b'dikoh*, as she is unable to insert the cloth deeep enough.   (R' Sh. Z. Auerbach *Zatzal*)

If a woman became *niddoh* on account of a *kesem* (see Ch. Fourteen), this extra longer lasting *b'dikoh* is not essential and should be omitted if *b'dikos* cause her problems.

In *Chutz Lo'oretz*, if the main *b'dikoh* was made on time but she did not start the additional *b'dikoh* before sunset, she should still attempt it (as long as it is still before night) and later on ask a *sha'aloh*. This does not apply in *Eretz Yisroel*.

On Shabbos

One must not walk in the street while the cloth is inserted in a place where one is not permitted to carry on *Shabbos*.

CHAPTER FIVE

THE SECOND STEP TOWARDS TA'HAROH

שבעה נקיים

The Interval of Seven Clean Days (Shiv'oh N'kiyim)

An interval of seven consecutive *clean* days is required before *t'viloh* can take place. One ascertains by two daily internal examinations that there is no evidence of blood. The day *following* the *hef'sek ta'haroh* examination is counted as the first of the seven clean days. The *niddoh* status is as yet unchanged with regard to conduct between husband and wife.

Twice Daily Examinations

On each of the seven days she makes one *b'dikoh* in the morning after dawn (soon after getting up[1]), and one in the

---

1. after washing her hands three times.

evening, before[2] sunset. These examinations are done *without* washing the body beforehand, she also examines her underwear. In winter the second examination may have to be made in the middle of the afternoon due to the short days. If she is unable to be at home near sunset, she should perform the examination earlier on in the afternoon before leaving home, unless there will be a possibility of making the *b'dikoh* at the correct time.

Note: If *t'viloh* did not take place at the normal time but was postponed for one or more days, no further examinations should be made after the seventh day.

Successful Examinations

If *all* examinations during these seven days are *clean* she will be able to go for *t'viloh* after the seventh day. (Some women have the *minhag* to say each day after successful examinations "today is the first, or the second, or the third day etc.".)

Doubtful Examinations

If upon inspection of the cloth on any of the seven clean days, a coloured stain, however small is noticed, or if a stain is noticed on underwear or bed linen, a *sha'aloh* is necessary. In the meantime, the two daily examinations should be continued, in case the *sha'aloh* will be declared *clean*.

Note: It is a common error that anything that can be easily removed from the examination cloth is counted *clean*. This is not necessarily true. Only a *Rav* can decide this.

---

2. If sunset passed, one should still make a *b'dikoh* as long as it is still before nightfall. This does not apply in the case of the *hef'sek ta'haroh b'dikoh*.

Unsuccessful Examination

If there was a distinct red mark on the cloth or if the *Rav* decided that the colour on the cloth shown to him was "not good", *all* previous days are invalidated, and the procedure of Chapter Four i.e. washing and examining before sunset must be repeated. After that one would attempt to count a new set of *seven clean days*.

If the negative result of a *sha'aloh* was not known until the following day (or later) but she had continued making *b'dikos* before that, she should consult a Rav, as to whether any of these *b'dikos* could be valid for *hef'sek ta'haroh*.

Omission of Examination

If one or more of the fourteen examinations of the seven days were missed, she may nevertheless continue counting, provided that apart from the *hef'sek ta'haroh b'dikoh*, at least one *b'dikoh* was made on the first and one on the last of the seven days. In any case a *sha'aloh* should be asked.

Difficulties in Accomplishing Seven Clean Days

Should there be continuous difficulties in successfully counting seven consecutive clean days or if there are physical difficulties e.g. pain, a *Rav* should be consulted.

ABOUT ASKING A SHA'ALOH

1) A woman should never hesitate asking a *sha'aloh* even if she fears that she may appear foolish.

2) She should not ask friends, neighbours, her mother or sister but only an experienced *Madrichah* who will guide her as to whether the problem warrants a *sha'aloh* or not.

3) If she asked a *sha'aloh* once and an identical case arises,
    she must ask again and not compare one case to the other.

4) A *sha'aloh* which was *paskened* as "not good" by one *Rav*
    must not be taken to a second *Rav* in the hope that he may
    say that is O.K., for, even if he would say so, the decision
    of the first *Rav* would stand.

5) If a woman has a *sha'aloh* about any of the *ta'haroh* laws,
    or on a doubtful *b'dikoh*, there are various ways how to set
    about it. One way is for her husband to present the
    sha'aloh to the *Rav*. Where this is not possible e.g. the
    sha'aloh needs to be resolved immediately, she could send
    the examination cloth to the *Rav*'s wife who will then pass
    it on to the *Rav*, or, where this is not possible, she herself
    could ask the *Rav* directly (as Rabbonim are used to these
    kinds of questions). *T'znius* wrongly applied is not a
    mitzvoh and could lead to problems. A *sha'aloh* may also
    be sent by post or put into the post-box of the *Rav*
    together with essential details such as at what stage the
    sha'aloh occurred e.g. at *hef'sek ta'haroh* or during the
    seven clean days or otherwise, with some form of
    identification (one's name or a number). One telephones
    later for the decision.

    If the *sha'aloh* concerns the *t'viloh* and she is already in the
    Mikveh, the easiest way would be by telephone. Asking a
    sha'aloh by telephone is sometimes unavoidable, as in this
    case, but should be avoided generally.

    Note: Some *sha'alos* are complicated and allowance should
    be made for time needed by the *Rav* in arriving at the
    correct decision.

CHAPTER SIX

PREPARING FOR T'VILOH

חפיפה

T'viloh in a *mikveh* is the essential and final act that brings about *ta'haroh*. It takes place at nightfall following the last of the *seven clean days* (i.e. at the beginning of the eighth day).

A *mikveh* - often called ritualarium or ritual bath - contains individual bathrooms and the *mikveh* pool. The *mikveh* pool is embedded in the ground and is joined to an underground store of rain, spring or sea water collected under special conditions. Through this we consider the *mikveh* to be a *natural* collection of water, which brings about the purifying quality of the *mikveh*. The appearance of the *mikveh* is comparable to a miniature swimming pool: five or six steps leading to a tiled cube-shaped area filled with fresh warm water reaching below shoulder height.

Note: A swimming pool itself is *not kosher* for use as a *mikveh*.

Modern *mikvaos*[1] are well equipped with hair dryers etc. A Jewish woman is in attendance.

Precautions on the Day of *T'viloh*

A woman must be *completely* clean at the time of her *t'viloh* (i.e. there must be no חציצה). She must take care therefore, not to handle adhesive substances e.g. grease, paste, plasticine, glue or paint etc. on the day of *t'viloh*, as these are hard to wash off.

Kneading dough or scraping off scales from fish should also be avoided as these are difficult to remove. These activities are permitted when preparing food for *Shabbos* or *Yom Tov*.

She must also refrain from eating meat since meat becomes easily lodged between the teeth (but soup is allowed). The exception to this is on *Shabbos, Yom Tov, Chol Ha'moed, Purim* or on the occasion of a proper *Se'udas Mitzvoh* e.g. a *bris miloh* or a wedding dinner.

On Friday or *Yom Tov* night, when all the preparations were made before *Shabbos* or *Yom Tov*, she refrains from eating until she comes home from the *t'viloh*. If this is causing problems, a *Rav* should be consulted. These restrictions do not apply to a woman who has no teeth and uses removable dentures.

If she forgot and handled adhesive substances or ate meat, *t'viloh* need not be postponed, but she must take extra care to clean very well her hands or mouth.

Note: The *b'dikoh* on the afternoon of the seventh day should not be forgotten.

---

1. Colloquially referred to as mikves!

The Preparations for *T'viloh*

These consist of: washing and combing the hair, having a bath, cleaning the teeth, cutting the nails and removing all intervening substances (חציצה). There is no special order in which these should be done.

Hair

a) All hairbands and clips etc. must be removed, and the hair must be washed with warm water and soap or shampoo.

b) Cold[2] water must not be used for washing the hair either at this stage or later.

c) The hair must be thoroughly rinsed in order to wash out all soap and lather.

d) The hair must be combed *while it is still wet* by using a strong, fairly fine comb until the hair is completely clean and free of all knots and tangles. Ample time must be allowed for this.

e) It is customary not to cut the hair of the head on the day of *t'viloh* out of fear that some loose hair may cause a *chatzitzoh*.

f) People who have lice should apply the recommended lotions the day before and comb out the nits etc. after applying the lotion. The hair should be washed and combed again shortly before *t'viloh* in the hope of freeing the hair of all nits. Ideally, this should be done by another person as this is more effective. If this is not a practical proposition, or if she would feel embarrassed about it, she herself should comb out the bulk of it until she feels that 'if it

---

2. As cold water tends to entangle hair.

would not be for the sake of *t'viloh* she herself would not care about it anymore'.

Nose and Ears

a)   Ear-rings must be removed.

b)   The ears have to be thoroughly cleaned. Ear wax or nasal discharge should be wiped away, but it is not necessary to clean the upper part of the nasal passage.

c)   If the inner part of the ear needs protection from water for medical reasons guidance must be sought from a *Rav*.

Eyes

a)   Contact lenses must be taken out.

b)   Eye shadow and other types of make-up must be removed.

c)   The inside and outside corners of both eyes must be cleaned (inside and outside) to ensure removal of possible eye discharge.

d)   Eye lashes and brows must be examined and manipulated and if necessary, washed several times to ensure that no hairs are stuck together.

Face and Mouth

a)   Make-up must be removed from face and lips.

b)   Teeth have to be brushed and cleaned with a toothpick, dental floss or a thread. One must take care that these do not get stuck between the teeth. If they did, they *must* be removed. *Absolutely nothing* must be left stuck between the teeth. Dentures must be removed. If they were not removed, she must *tovel* a second time after their removal.

c)   If a woman is under dental care and has a temporary filling a *sha'aloh* must be asked before going to *t'viloh*.

Fingers and Toes

a)   All rings must be removed.

b)   Nail varnish must be removed; if it was removed previously but some traces of varnish still remained, these must now be completely removed.

c)   Finger and toe nails must be cut as short as practical[3] and after that thoroughly cleaned. Loose skin around nails need to be cut off, but corns and hard skin need not and should not[4].

The usual cleaning process, including the cutting of nails is done even during the *nine days*[5] or on *Chol Ha'moed*. During the thirty days of mourning, (*sh'loshim*) i.e. after the *shiv'oh*[6] the nails should preferably be cut by another woman.

d)   If [even] one nail was not cut before *t'viloh*, *t'viloh* needs to be repeated without a *b'rochoh*, after cutting the nail.

e)   If she is unable to cut a nail on account of a swelling, the accessible part below the nail should be cleaned.

---

3. As it is difficult to clean them *perfectly* without cutting.
4. As this leads often to more skin becoming loose causing a vicious circle. One should not use a brush for the sole of the foot as this could also cause skin to become loose.
5. i.e. the nine days preceding *tish'oh b'Av*.
6. Note: *T'viloh* must not take place during the *Shiv'oh*.

f)   A splinter or other foreign object, however small, stuck in the flesh must be removed, unless it is lodged *entirely* below the surface of the skin.

g)   The feet should be well-washed, especially between the toes.

The following cases are subject to a *sha'aloh*:

i)   If a nail can be neither cut nor cleaned on account of a swollen finger.

ii)   If a woman cut *into* a nail and there is a gap between the two parts of the nail.

iii) When *t'viloh* takes place on Friday night and she forgot to cut a nail.

iv)   If she became aware only on the next day that she did not cut a nail (i.e. she should *not tovel* again without asking a *sha'aloh* first).

The Body

a)   She must wash all parts of her body with warm water and soap, including the body folds, the naval and the intimate parts.

b)   If she has a ring or anything else inserted within her body for medical reasons, she must ask a *sha'aloh*.

c)   All body hair e.g. under the arms, must be washed and manipulated to make sure that it is clean and that no hairs are stuck together.

After the bath she should rinse herself with fresh warm water to ensure that all lather has been removed, especially from the hair.

INTERVENING SUBSTANCES (חציצה)

Plasters and Adhesive Substances

Plasters, bandages and all other substances e.g. ointments or paints, must be removed. In the case of plasters care must be taken to remove all traces of adhesive. Ink or paint marks need special attention.

Wounds

a) If there is a fresh cut or wound which is still bleeding, *t'viloh* may take place, but not if there is dried or sticky blood (see c).

b) Pus which drained from a wound within three days of the *t'viloh* (72 hours), is not considered a *chatzitzoh*; but it is customary to remove it, if this is possible. If it drained from the wound more than three days before *t'viloh*, the pus *must* be removed. This can be achieved by first bathing it in warm water until it is soft. It is then removed.

c) Dried or sticky blood of a cut or a wound must be removed by bathing it in warm water.

d) If there is a scratch a *sha'aloh* should be asked. If there is a scab (i.e. which protects the wound and eventually falls off when the fresh skin grows underneath) *t'viloh* may take place.

Stitches

If she has had stitches for a wound or an operation and these were not yet removed, a *Rav* must be consulted.

TIME OF GOING TO THE MIKVEH

The major part of the preparation should take place ideally before nightfall so that *t'viloh* can take place shortly after nightfall. Approximately one hour should be allowed for the total preparations. Slow women, should also try to manage within an hour[7].

A *mikveh* which serves a large community cannot always accommodate everyone before nightfall. Some women will prefer therefore to make part or all preparations at home, shortly before leaving for the *mikveh*.

When preparations are made at home, she must take care after bathing not to touch anything that could adhere to the skin. She must not apply cosmetics, deodorants or hairspray. When she arrives at the *mikveh* it is customary to rinse her body and hair with warm water and to do some combing (while the hair is wet) before the *t'viloh*.

If it is not practical for a woman to make her preparations before nightfall because she is at work or needs to look after her children etc., she may delay them (exceptionally) until after nightfall. As a matter of fact she would *not be allowed* to miss her regular employment in order to go to the *mikveh* an hour before nightfall, due to her financial obligation towards her employer.

It is permitted to delay going to the *mikveh* until after nightfall out of *tzni'us* considerations i.e. if people would suspect

---

7. Sitting for a long time in a bath can be very tiring, especially in the late evenings and there are good reasons why she should spare her strength this night. This applies especially to pregnant women who have to go to *t'viloh*. They should not sit for a long time in a hot bath as this may cause a miscarriage.

why she is missing.[8] If a woman goes to the *mikveh* only after nightfall, extra care must be taken not to carry out the preparations in a hurry!

అంఙఞ⅛ఞఞ

---

8. This would not be a consideration, if she lives with her parents or other very close relations.

CHAPTER SEVEN

T'VILOH

THE FINAL STEP TOWARDS TA'HAROH

הטבילה

a)   *T'viloh* must not take place before nightfall.

b)   Even if *t'viloh* is postponed to the eighth day, or later, it may not take place during daytime, under normal circumstances.

c)   In exceptional circumstances e.g. if there is no *mikveh* in the place where she lives and she has to travel to another town and it would be too late to return home the same night, or if it is not safe to be out after dark even when accompanied by her husband (who could otherwise wait for her near the *mikveh*), *t'viloh* may take place during daytime from the eighth day onwards, but *not on the seventh day* (even if her husband would not be in town until after night).

d)   If *t'viloh* takes place during daytime on the eighth day (or later), she must delay her return home until after nightfall if her husband would be in the house at that time.

Check-up Before *T'viloh*

a)   A final check is made to see that the whole body including her back is clean. This is done visually and by touch (on the parts of the body which cannot be seen). In some places the attendant assists in the checking.

If a woman realises after *t'viloh*, that the check-up was omitted, her *t'viloh* is not valid. A check-up, plus another *t'viloh* is necessary.[1] If only part of the check-up was omitted a *sha'aloh* is necessary.

b)   In order to be relaxed during *t'viloh* she should go to the toilet beforehand. If this was omitted the *t'viloh* is kosher.

c)   Care should be taken on the way from the bathroom to the *mikveh*-pool that nothing adheres to the soles of her feet.

The *T'viloh*

She descends the steps of the *mikveh*-pool until the water level is approximately 30 cm[2] above the naval when standing up (or a span i.e. from the tip of the thumb to the tip of the little finger when the hand and fingers are stretched out). This height will enable her to *tovel* without bending forward or ducking too

---

1. Even if she had gone home already
2. If it is less than 30 cm high and there is no way of adding water, 24 cm would suffice.

much. The water level should also not be much higher than 30 cm,[3] because of the tendency of water to lift a person and that would result in her not being in full control of her posture at the time of immersion. (See further on "Posture")

Very tall women[4] may occasionally find that even when standing at the deep end the water level is not high enough. If the attendant is authorised to add water she should ask for this.

She then immerses once recites the *b'rochoh*, and immerses a second[5] time. The *b'rochoh*[6] is said while she is in the water. She places her arms below her heart,[7] looks out of the water, makes sure not to face any women going to or coming out of the water,[8] and says: בָּרוּךְ אַתָּה ה' אֱלֹהֵינוּ מֶלֶךְ הָעוֹלָם אֲשֶׁר קִדְּשָׁנוּ בְּמִצְוֹתָיו וְצִוָּנוּ עַל הַטְּבִילָה.

---

3. i.e. not up to her neck.
4. Such women should ask a *sha'aloh* in advance how to *toi'vel* if the water level would not be high enough.
5. Many women have a custom to immerse three times. One should say on the first time before the third *t'viloh* that one accepts it *bli' neder* (i.e. not as a vow).
6. If the need for *t'viloh* was caused by a *doubtful* colour or by any other *doubt* it is more correct not to say a *b'rochoh*.
7. Preferably without her hands touching her body.
8. In some very busy *mikvaos, complete* privacy is impossible at times. Someone who is particular about this should choose a *mikveh* where complete privacy can be guaranteed, or arrange a time when each person is attended to individually. It should be noted, however, that it is not considered a lack of *tzni'us* if full privacy cannot be achieved. It can be argued furthermore, that it is a *Kidush Hashem* that so many women flock to the *mikveh* to fulfill this beautiful and elevating *mitzvoh* which is the key to the holiness of our people. But it would be better if there were more *mikvaos* as full privacy *is* preferable for many other good reasons. *T'viloh* is a very emotional time and thoughts of jealousy on seeing women with better *mazol* should best be avoided, especially at this time. Imagine how a woman who has no children feels at seeing a woman with a large family at that very time!

Posture

She immerses in a relaxed position - the body bent slightly forward, the legs a little apart and the arms slightly raised in order that *all* parts of her body come into contact with the water simultaneously. If she was too erect or if she ducked too low, or bent too much forward, immersion should be repeated preferably.

Legs and Arms

The legs, arms and fingers should neither press against one another nor against her body. If they did, the *t'viloh* must be performed again.

Eyes and Mouth

The face should be relaxed, the eyes and mouth gently closed; the lips may touch one another but without pressing. If the eyes or mouth were closed too tightly the *t'viloh* must be performed again.

Hair

A *t'viloh* is not valid unless the whole body i.e. all limbs and every hair are immersed below the surface of the water *at the same time*. Great care should be taken, therefore, to bend to an adequate depth, for *even if one hair were not covered with water the t'viloh would not be valid*. Women with long[9] hair have to be especially careful about this. (See next paragraph)

---

9. Some women prefer to keep their hair relatively short so that no complications arise at the *t'viloh*.

Supervision of *T'viloh*

To ensure that *t'viloh* is done in accordance with the *din* and that *all* hair is covered by water the *t'viloh* must be supervised. This is usually done by the attendant. If the attendant finds it difficult to see whether *all* hair was in fact under the surface of the water or if the *mikveh* is not adequately lit[10] and the *t'viloh* cannot be satisfactorily supervised, the hair must be kept down by a loose-fitting hair net. This may be necessary in any case for a woman[11] who has exceptionally long hair, as one should not bend forward or downwards too much. See page 34 - "Posture". *A net is therefore an essential piece of equipment for every mikveh.*

Doubtful *T'viloh*

a) If a woman notices after *t'viloh* that a foreign matter adheres to her body or that she forgot to remove a ring or false teeth etc. or if a doubt arises regarding the proper execution of one of the preparatory or *t'viloh* laws (e.g. if the cutting of a nail was overlooked), this must be corrected immediately, followed by another *t'viloh* without a *b'rochoh*.

b) If the doubt arises *after* she left for home she should ask a *sha'aloh* as to whether a second *t'viloh* is necessary. If it is not possible to ask a *sha'aloh* she has *no* alternative but to repeat the *t'viloh*. If the doubt was not realised until the following day a *sha'aloh* is essential i.e. she should not *toi'vel* again on her own accord without consulting a *Rav*.

---

10. e.g. there is an electrical fault, or when *t'viloh* takes place on *Shabbos* and the light was not left on.
11. e.g. a *Kalloh* with very long hair.

T'viloh - A Private Matter

T'viloh is something very personal and private. As far as possible, no outsider should know that it will take place or that it has taken place unless advice or assistance is required or a *sha'aloh* needs to be asked.

On Coming Home

A woman should always inform her husband that she has been to *t'viloh*. (See Conduct of *Tzni'us* for Husband and Wife - See Part II Chapter Two)

Some women have the habit of giving money to charity on the night of *t'viloh*.

A *T'filloh*[12]

It is appropriate to say this t'filloh or at least the first part of it on the night of t'viloh. One may prefer to say the Hebrew text on Pages ג - ב.

Ribonoh Shel Olom (Master of the Universe!) Let us merit to beget good children and that our children should shine with *Torah*; that they be healthy in body and spirit; that they be clever and possess worthy *middos* and a love for the study of *Torah*.

Please, oh please, grant them a long and good life! Will it that they devote their life to the study of Your holy *Torah*, that they be wise and full of *Yir'as Shoma'yim*, and that they be loved by You and by their fellowmen. Save them from evil eyes, from all kinds of punishments and from the clutches of their *Yetzer Horah* (bad inclinations) but, instead bless them with good inclinations. (end of first part)

In Your great mercy, grant me and my wife/husband long life blessed with (mutual) love and peace and all good things and *nachas*. Grant

---

12. This *T'filloh* should be said often, and especially at the *Kosel*.

us to bring up each one of our children to *Torah*, to *Chuppoh* and to good deeds.

Merciful G-d, cause it to happen that each of our children will meet the partner in marriage which was bestowed for him or for her in the right time and while they are still young. Bless us so that we shall be able to promise them *bli neder* a generous dowry and to fulfill our promises.

Let us have the merit to see them getting married with *nachas* and joy and let them merit to have children who will be *tzadikim* and who will contribute to the welfare of *Klal Yisroel*.

May it be Your will that no one of our family and none of our descendants will ever defile Your holy name, *chas vesholom*.

Please, fulfill all our requests in good health and with beneficial success. May Your great name and the honour of Your *Torah* be glorified through us and through our children and descendants for ever. Omen! May this be Your will.

May my words and thoughts find acceptance with You, G-d My Rock and My Redeemer.

SUMMARY: FROM HEF'SEK TA'HAROH TO T'VILOH

(CHAPTERS FOUR TO SEVEN)

A. Examination on or after fifth day (*Hef'sek Ta'haroh*)

1) Count the day on which the period started plus four days (i.e. a minimum of five[13] days) and make an examination on or after the fifth day.

2) This examination (*b'dikoh*) takes place before sunset.

3) First wash with warm water to remove all traces of blood. Then take a suitable *examination* cloth (i.e. a soft, white, clean, absorbent material), wrap it around the forefinger and insert finger with cloth into the vagina - as deep as possible. Press cloth around all sides by turning the finger into one and then the other direction.

4) Examine the cloth by daylight to see whether it is perfectly clean, with no traces of red, pink, brown, yellow, orange, black or gray.

5) If the examination was not entirely satisfactory, you may attempt another examination as long as it is before sunset. If the second attempt was also not clean postpone the examination for a day or two and follow the routine of 2), 3) & 4).

6) If the result was *clean*, change to fresh *white* underwear. Then make a further longer-lasting examination (*b'dikoh*) by inserting, still before sunset, a cloth which is left inserted until nightfall. Inspect the cloth in the night but again next morning by *daylight*. If it is *clean* you may start counting the *seven clean days* as preparation for *t'viloh*.

---

13. According to *minhag* of *s'fardim* six days.

7)   Spread fresh *white* sheets on your bed.

B. Seven Clean Days

1)   Make two daily examinations for seven days, one in the
       morning and one before sunset. All examinations must have
       clean results. The cloth must always be inspected by
       daylight. If there is a red mark on the cloth, even on the
       sixth or seventh day, *all* days are invalidated and one must
       start afresh [see (a) numbers 2-6]. If you are in doubt
       concerning the colour ask a *sha'aloh*. Blood found on the
       underwear or bed linen requires a *sha'aloh*.

C. Preparing for *T'viloh*

1)   On the day before *t'viloh* takes place (i.e. the seventh day)
       take care not to handle adhesive substances, e.g. glue or
       dough. Also eat no meat (except on *Shabbos* or *Yom Tov*).

2)   Allow about an hour for the preparations before
       immersion.

3)   *The preparations:* Cut short the nails of fingers and toes;
       brush and clean teeth so that absolutely nothing remains
       stuck between the teeth; remove everything removable e.g.
       rings, ear-rings, hair clips, contact lenses, nail varnish,
       make-up, plasters, cotton wool (absorbing cotton) from
       ears and anything that adheres to the body; have a
       thorough bath and comb hair while it is wet, *after* washing
       it with warm water; comb the hair until it is free of all
       knots and tangles and of excessive dandruff; clean ears,
       nose and corners of eyes.

4)   If you are unable to clean some areas as required or if you
       have a wound with dry blood or pus, ask a *sha'aloh*.

The Immersion (*t'viloh*)

1) *T'viloh* takes place after night fall.

2) *Final check-up:* Check whether you are completely clean and whether all soap has been removed, especially from hair. This check-up is often done with the assistance of the *mikveh* attendant.

3) Go down the steps of the *mikveh* pool until the water reaches approximately half way between the naval and the chin. Then dip below the surface of the water in a *relaxed* position - the body bent slightly forward, the arms slightly raised, the legs a little apart and the eyes and mouth gently closed. Do not press arms or fingers against one another or against the body. Take great care that *all* hair is below the surface of the water.

4) *T'viloh* must be supervised so that it is certain that the whole body, hands and hair are below the surface of the water. After one immersion make the *b'rochoh*: ברוך אתה ה' אלהינו מלך העולם אשר קדשנו במצותיו וצונו על הטבילה.

5) During the *b'rochoh* place arms below the heart and look out of the water. After the *b'rochoh* immerse a second time.

CHAPTER EIGHT

T'VILOH ON SHABBOS OR YOM TOV

T'viloh at the appropriate time (i.e. if it was not unnecessarily delayed), may take place on *Shabbos* or *Yom Tov*, but the preparations such as bathing, combing hair and cutting nails must be made *beforehand*.

Ideally, the preparations should be made in the *mikveh* as usual. One needs to go early so that there will be sufficient time before the commencement of *Shabbos* or *Yom Tov* to carry out the preparations with the usual care and patience. She must then wait until nightfall to immerse.

If it is impossible to leave the house on account of domestic or other considerations, the preparations may be made in the house and she would go to the *mikveh* only for the *t'viloh* which will take place after nightfall. After completing the preparations, she must take care not to handle any sticky foodstuffs and, when she lights the candles, not to touch melted wax. If she needs to serve food to her family or to attend to a baby she should try to remain clean. She should wash[1] her hands nevertheless, so that nothing adheres to them. Her own meal is postponed until after *t'viloh*. If there would be a very long wait or if there will be other people eating with them, she should ask a *sha'aloh* in advance whether an exception may be made.

Lighting Candles

If possible, she should light the candles herself after the preparations at the usual time and accept *Shabbos*. Should this not prove practical there are two alternatives:

a) Her husband lights the candles.

b) She lights the candles earlier than usual, *before* the preparations, and says explicitly before lighting the candles or has in mind, that she does not yet accept *Shabbos*. She would need to take care to stop *melochos* later on before the official time of *kabolas Shabbos* (i.e. the published time).

On *Yom Tov* the candles may be lit after nightfall upon returning home by lighting the candles from a source of fire prepared before *Yom Tov*.[2]

The *T'viloh*

The usual check-up is made before the *t'viloh* (see Page 32). When she dries herself she must take care not to squeeze her hair, but she may put a towel on her hair without applying pressure.

---

1. Preferably with warm water.
2. See "Guide to the laws of *Yom Tov*" Page 20 by the same author.

Preparations Not Finished In Time

a)   If time is short she should concentrate before *Shabbos* on the essentials and later do what is permitted on *Shabbos*.

If some essential preparations were not completed by the time *Shabbos* or *Yom Tov* commenced, *t'viloh* may have to be postponed until after *Shabbos* or *Yom Tov*.

b)   Essentials which may not be done after commencement of *Shabbos* are: washing and combing of hair, cutting nails, having a bath or even washing the greater part of the body. The same applies on *Yom Tov*, except that one may wash on *Yom Tov* even the whole body with warm water (heated before *Yom Tov*) provided that the parts of the body are not all washed simultaneously but first one and then the other and so on (but not the hair).

c)   Preparations permitted on *Shabbos* or *Yom Tov*: cleaning the nose, ears, eyes and mouth without a wet cloth or wet absorbing cotton (cotton-wool), manipulating hair or washing only part of the body, but she must go out of the bath once *Shabbos* comes in.

If necessary, a *dry* tooth brush without toothpaste may be used gently to avoid bleeding.

In any case, care must be taken with the following:

i)   not to use: a cloth or flannel, sponge or solid soap. Liquid soap is permitted;

ii)   pieces of dry absorbing cotton (cotton wool) may be used only if they were prepared before *Shabbos* or *Yom Tov*;

iii) hot water must normally not be obtained from a supply of running hot water[3];

iv)   cleaning the teeth must be done with care in order not to cause bleeding of the gums;

v)   hair must not be combed or squeezed;

vi)   a comb, a piece of soap, a sponge, and a face cloth are *muktzeh*;

One may ask a non-Jew[4] to do a *melochoh* until a few minutes *before* nightfall, e.g. if she forgot to cut a nail or did not comb her hair.

Unlit *Mikveh* on Shabbos

In a case of a *mikveh* which is not lit it would be permitted to ask a non-Jew to switch on the light, as long as it is still before nightfall, even though *Shabbos* has already commenced.

After nightfall, if there is complete darkness, she may perform *t'viloh* under the following conditions, that:-

i)   a satisfactory check-up can be made by another woman in a place where there is a light, or if she can check herself by feeling all parts of her body with her hands that there is no *chatzitzoh*;

ii)   safeguards to ensure complete immersion are taken by her wearing a loose-fitting net[5] — preferably made from nylon

---

3. This would depend on the type of hot water system in use and the attendant should be consulted.

4. Busy *mikvaos* should consider whether it would be a practical proposition to employ a non-Jewish woman for such eventualities, and less busy *mikvaos* should have a non-Jewish person on call.

5. Care must be taken not to squeeze the net after it becomes wet. Once she removes it, the net is to be treated as *muktzeh* until it dries.

— to cover her hair and by her immersing well below
water level;

iii)   she is not nervous or frightened (for she would then not be
relaxed the way she should be at the time of immersion);

iv)   the woman who supervises will be able to satisfy herself
that complete immersion took place. The supervising
woman may have to go herself into the water in order to be
able to feel with her hands that the woman who *toveled*
was completely covered by the water, if this cannot be
achieved otherwise.

CHAPTER NINE

T'VILOH AFTER: SHABBOS, YOM TOV, TISH'OH B'AV OR YOM KIPPUR

On *Motzei Shabbos* or *Yom Tov*

a) If the night of *t'viloh* falls on *Motzei Shabbos* or *Motzei Yom Tov*, the woman should make all her usual preparations on *Erev Shabbos* or *Erev Yom Tov.*[1]

b) As far as possible she should try to avoid touching sticky foodstuffs or anything that could soil her hands during *Shabbos*. If contact is unavoidable she should wash her hands immediately.

1. Since under normal circumstances the main preparations before *t'viloh* must be done during daytime (see Page 29).

c)   She may eat meat at the *Shabbos* or *Yom Tov* meals.[2]

d)   The twice daily examinations are performed in the usual way on *Shabbos* and *Yom Tov.*

e)   She brushes her teeth again prior to the *t'viloh*, has a bath and combs her hair while it is wet, but she need not spend as much time on this as she would on other days.

On *Motzei Tish'oh B'Av* & *Motzei Yom Kippur*

The same routine as for *Motzei Shabbos* is followed. (See previous paragraphs) i.e. the preparations are done in advance on *Erev Tish'oh B'Av* or *Erev Yom Kippur.*

If *t'viloh* is due on *Kol Nidre* or *Tish'oh B'Av* night, *t'viloh* is postponed until *Motzei Yom Kippur* or *Motzei Tish'oh B'Av* respectively, but the preparations are done in advance, as on *Erev Shabbos.* There is no need for *b'dikos* on *Tish'oh B'Av* or *Yom Kippur* in this case as they occur on the eighth day.

On Second Night of *Yom Tov;*[3] *Yom Tov* Night following *Shabbos*; *Shabbos* following *Yom Tov*

a)   The common factor of all these cases is that the usual preparations of bathing etc. must not take place on the night of *t'viloh* and for that the main preparations are made in advance, on *Erev Shabbos* or *Erev Yom Tov* respectively.

---

2. In honour of *Shabbos* or *Yom Tov.*

3. On *Motzei Shabbos* which is preceded by two days of *Yom Tov* (i.e. *Yom Tov* fell on Thursday and Friday), and *t'viloh* falls on *Motzei Shabbos,* or when *Shabbos* is followed by two days of *Yom Tov* and *t'viloh* falls on *Motzei Yom Tov* a *Sha'aloh* should be asked concerning the preparations to be done.

b)   To maintain the effects of combing i.e. that the hair does not become entangled, one covers it overnight with a net and protects it during the day.

c)   Contact should be avoided[4] with greasy or sticky food or anything that might soil her. If contact is unavoidable she should wash immediately.

d)   Meat may be eaten.

The following is done prior to *t'viloh*:

She cleans her mouth and teeth and takes care not to cause the gums to bleed. She washes and checks her hands and fingernails carefully and, if necessary, cleans them. Care must be taken not to pull off loose skin. She rinses body folds, her under arms and intimate parts with warm water, but must not use a cloth or a sponge. She cleans the eyes, nose and ears. She may wash only the smaller part of her body as it would be considered otherwise like having a bath. The usual check-up prior to *t'viloh* must be made with special care. (See Page 32)

See Chapters Eight and Nine regarding the *dinim* of *tovelling* on *Shabbos* or *Yom Tov*.

---

4. Rubber gloves could be used.

CHAPTER TEN

T'VILOH
ON TIME

מצות טבילה בזמנה

It is a woman's marital obligation and privilege to go to *t'viloh* at the correct time. She must not delay her preparations for the *seven clean days* and for her *t'viloh* even for one day. She must certainly not decide on her own to miss *t'viloh* for one or two months even if she would keep the *niddoh* law. An exception is if she is unwell or weak and finds it difficult to go to *t'viloh*. If her husband is out of town, it is customary to go to *t'viloh* only near the time that he is expected home, unless there is a chance that he *may* come home earlier.

Not to wash within three days

For three days after marital relations have taken place a woman should not wash her intimate parts or sit in a bath, especially after the *t'viloh* night, as this may prevent her from becoming pregnant. It is recommended, also, that she walks little on these three days and rests as much as possible.[1]

After Childbirth

Many factors have to be considered after childbirth in deciding how long[2] a rest the wife requires before going to *t'viloh*. These include the husband and wife's mutual considerations, the medical and *halochoh* considerations, and if necessary, medical and rabbinical advice should be sought.

If a prolonged rest from child-bearing is required on medical grounds, then they should consult a *Rav* concerning the possibility of *her* using some form of contraception for a limited[3] period.

Rabbonim do not permit use of contraception for the husband, although this is the safest method.

Note: The wife must not use any form of contraception *at any time* without both the consent of her husband and rabbinical permission - be it the Pill or otherwise.[4]

Summary:

1.   *T'viloh* must not be postponed unless there are extraordinary circumstances.

2.   Contraception must not be used unless health problems arise. A *Rav* should be consulted.

---

1. These hints are based on *Chazal* and on common sense, but should not be taken as an alternative to medical consultations but rather in conjunction with their recommendations.
2. Whether at least 6 weeks or longer, depending on how strong she is and on how a fresh pregnancy would affect her.
3. A *he'ter* may be given by a *Rav* for a limited period. After that, if there are still health problems, they must ask a sha'aloh again.
4. For further details see *Taharas Am Yisroel* Part One, Chapter Seven.

CHAPTER ELEVEN

HOW A
WOMAN
BECOMES
NIDDOH

The most common cause for becoming *niddoh* is the onset of the menstrual period, but any issue of blood renders a woman a *niddoh*.

If a woman suspects that her period has begun she must inform her husband and investigate as soon as she has the opportunity and, if necessary, make an internal examination. If a red mark, however small, is noticed she is *niddoh*.

The date and time of day i.e. whether by day[1] or by night[2] should be recorded[3] in her private (Jewish) calendar.

---

1. Between sunrise and sunset. If the period started near sunrise or sunset exact timing is imperative.
2. Between sunset and sunrise.
3. If there were definite symptoms these should also be recorded (see Page 61).

Exact recording is important for the following reasons:

a)   to enable her to calculate the fifth day for the *hef'sek ta'haroh* examination (see page 9);

b)   to enable her to calculate when the next period is to be anticipated (see Chapter Thirteen).

Compulsory Investigation

The following cases require *immediate* investigation at any time:

1)   If a woman has a sensation similar to that felt at the beginning of a period even at a time when the period is not anticipated, she must check by an internal examination *and* by an inspection of the undergarments whether this can be attributed to a clean discharge or not. If nothing is found she may be *niddoh* nevertheless on the ground that there may have been a drop of blood which cannot be traced anymore. She should consult a *Rav*.

If this happened during pregnancy after the third month and nothing was found she remains clean, because issue of blood is then unlikely.

2)   If a woman feels a flow she must investigate whether it is blood or a clean discharge. If the discharge is untraceable a *sha'aloh* is required; during pregnancy (after the third month) she remains clean.

3)   A woman, who regularly finds clean discharges in the case of 1) & 2) should ask for rabbinical guidance whether investigations will be necessary on future occasions or whether she may assume a clean discharge.

Note: A woman who feels a discharge during the days when her period is expected, must *always* investigate, even if it was *paskened* that she need not make an examination at other times when she feels a discharge. (See 3.)

NIDDOH NOT DUE TO A PERIOD

All bleeding originating from the womb renders a woman a *niddoh*. Minute dots, hair-like or pin-head like substances found on an examination cloth are subject to a *sha'aloh* even if they could be removed. Blood found on her body or on her garments i.e. spotting or staining may render her a *niddoh*, depending on the conditions which will be explained in Chapter Fourteen.

Colours of discharge

All shades of red, pink, rose or black are not *clean*. Orange, brown, beige, yellow or similar colours require a *sha'aloh*.

Bleeding not due to a period may occur in the following instances: before and after childbirth; before or after a miscarriage; during pregnancy (this if often a sign of a threatened miscarriage[4]); after the insertion of a medical instrument into the womb;[5] as a result of an operation on the womb. In all cases she is a *niddoh*. If blood is found after a medical inspection a *sha'aloh* must be asked.

Internal Wounds

If one finds blood on an examination cloth, one must not assume automatically that it originates from a wound or sore, even if one has a sore. A *sha'aloh* must be asked.

---

4. If that would happen she should immediately go to bed and *not* go to see a doctor. A doctor should be called to come to the house. Lying in bed is the essential precaution in preventing a miscarriage. Many pregnancies have been saved in this way!

5. A *sha'aloh* is necessary irrespective of whether there was bleeding or not.

Bleeding Resulting from Marital Relationships

If bleeding is noticed shortly after marital relations the woman is a *niddoh*. An urgent *sha'aloh* must be asked as a recurrence may jeopardize the future of their marriage. For details concerning bleeding on the first few occasions after marriage see Chapter Seventeen Pages 78 - 81.

A woman who becomes a *niddoh* during intercourse, or if she became aware that she was a *niddoh* beforehand must inform her husband immediately. They must not part one from the other before he is fully relaxed. The woman should remain completely passive, and he should press his fingers and toes downwards and remove his body from her slightly until he is fully relaxed and separate only then. A *Rav* must be consulted.

Summary:

1.   When a period or flow is suspected an immediate investigation is obligatory.

2.   Any bleeding or red coloured discharge renders her a *niddoh*.

3.   The time of the onset of bleeding must be recorded.

CHAPTER TWELVE

MENSTRUATION DATES

פרישה סמוך לווסת

Menstruation dates are days on which the oncoming period is to be anticipated according to the calculations of *halochoh*. Precautionary separation is necessary on such days. Most women need to keep two or three menstruation dates every month i.e. the 30th and 31st day and the *same interval day*, as will be explained in detail in Chapters Thirteen, Nineteen and Twenty.

Menstruation dates must be kept in the following month irrespective of whether the previous bleeding was due to a period or to any other cause, even after bleeding during pregnancy. Blood which showed up as a result of a *b'dikoh* is also treated like a period in this respect, but not if bleeding was caused by an internal cause e.g. a medical examination (even if she would be considered as *tomeh)*. There is no need to keep menstruation dates after spotting, even if she had to conduct herself as *tomeh*.

Separation

Husband and wife must separate on *menstruation dates* even though she is not yet *niddoh*. They should refrain also from intimacies e.g. embracing, but need not observe total separation as during the *niddoh* period (see Chapter Fifteen); for example, they may pass objects from one to the other or touch the other if not done out of fondness, they may eat together without a reminder, but they must not sleep in one bed.

When To Separate

According to the strict letter of the law separation is required only during the day(s) or the night(s) of the anticipated period, i.e. the 30th and 31st day and the *same interval* day. It is widespread practice, however, to separate also on the previous day or night (i.e. a full day). If this extra separation would cause problems a *sha'aloh* should be asked.

Example: If the last period began in the morning or in the afternoon, separation takes place on *menstruation dates* during the daytime of the 30th and 31st day. According to some opinions, also during the previous nights.

Examination on Menstruation Dates For an Irregular Period

It is necessary to make one *b'dikoh* at least during each of the *menstruation dates* to find out whether the period has come or not.

If she plans to have a bath on the 30th day she should delay it until after the *b'dikoh*, as there is a greater chance that the period will come on this day.

Marital relations may be resumed after the *menstruation dates*, provided that there is no sign of the oncoming period.[1]

Examinations Omitted On Menstruation Dates

If all *menstruation dates* pass without any symptoms of an oncoming period, she remains *clean* even if she forgot to examine herself *on* the *menstruation dates*.[2] However, if the *b'dikoh* was missed also on the 30th day the resuming of marital relations would be permitted only after a *b'dikoh*.[3]

Examination on Menstruation Dates For a Regular Period

In the case of a woman who has a regular period *two* examinations must take place during[4] the day or night that her period is anticipated, the second one shortly before sunset or sunrise. She should delay taking a bath on that day until after the examinations. If she did have a bath, a *sha'aloh* is necessary whether the *b'dikoh* would still be effective. If no examination took place on the day a regular period was anticipated, it *must* be made after that day as soon[5] as possible.

Summary:

1. During the day(s) the period is anticipated husband and wife must separate.

2. She must examine herself on these days to find out whether the period has come or not.

---

1. It would be prudent in such a case to make one *b'dikoh* as an extra precaution shortly before and one shortly after marital relations, for the sake of one's peace of mind.
2. As we assume that she would have been aware of her menstruating if it had occurred.
3. As there may have been an issue of blood which was not noticed. The *b'dikoh* is necessary even if it was established that she is pregnant.
4. Depending on whether the period was due during the day or the night.
5. See footnote 3.

CHAPTER THIRTEEN

CALCULATING MENSTRUATION DATES

Until one is fully conversant with the complex of cycles (see Chapters Twenty-One and Twenty-Two) [1]most eventualities will be covered if one observes always three *menstruation dates* i.e. the 30th and 31st day[2] plus the date which corresponds to the interval between the last two periods, i.e. *the same-interval day*.

These are calculated in the following way:

Step I - Establishing the last two periods

Note the dates when the last *two* periods began by consulting your private calendar, i.e. P1 & P2   (See Chart on Page 61).

---

1. Except where the period is preceded by *definite* symptoms (See Page 61).
2. This takes care of the *lunar* and *thirty days* cycles (See Pages 86 & 87).

Step II - How to calculate the 30th and 31st day

Call the day on which the *last* period, i.e. P2, started, day one and mark the 30th and the 31st after that as menstruation dates.[3]

Example A: If the last period occurred on a Tuesday then the 30th and 31st day will fall on Wednesday and Thursday, respectively, four weeks after that period.

	S	M	T	W	Th	F	שבת
Week 1			P				
Week 2							
Week 3							
Week 4							
Week 5				30	31		

Step III - How to calculate the same-interval day

a)   Calculate the number of days between the start of the last two periods (both days inclusive; see *Step I*) i.e. between P1 & P2 (see chart on Page 61) to obtain the last *interval* and

b)   Count a corresponding number of days from P2, i.e. the day the *last period began (that day inclusive)*[4] and mark the resulting day as the expected *menstruation date*.[5]

---

3. Remember that the night belongs to the following day and that the *day* is counted from sunrise to sunset and the *night* from sunset to sunrise.

4. This takes care of the *same-interval* cycle (See Page 86).

5. In a case where the interval between the last two periods was shorter than the interval between earlier periods, the more stringent view is to take note *also* of this longer interval and separate on both days. According to this view, the longer interval is not considered as having been cancelled by a *short* interval.

Example B: If the *first* of the last two periods began on a Wednesday and the second one on Tuesday after an interval of 28 days (both days being inclusive), then the next menstruation date will fall after an interval of 28 days after that Tuesday i.e. on Monday.

	S	M	T	W	Th	F	שבת
Week 1				P1 1	2	3	4
Week 2	5	6	7	8	9	10	11
Week 3	12	13	14	15	16	17	18
Week 4	19	20	21	22	23	24	25
Week 5	26	27	28 P21	2	3	4	5
Week 6	6	7	8	9	10	11	12
Week 7	13	14	15	16	17	18	19
Week 8	20	21	22	23	24	25	26
Week 9	27	28	29	30	31		

To summarize, in this example the woman will observe three days: Monday (the 28th day), Wednesday (the 30th day) and Thursday (the 31st day).

A Regular Pattern

If after studying the pattern of one's periods a regular pattern of three consecutive periods is recognised i.e. three equal dates of the Jewish calendar e.g. 5th Nissan, 5th Iyar, 5th Sivan or three equal intervals e.g. 28 days, 28 days, 28 days, or three identical days of the week, rabbinical guidance would be required to plan out future *menstruation dates*. (See Chapter Twenty for guidance concerning *regular* periods.)

Period Preceded by Symptoms

A woman who has on the day the period starts definite symptoms, which indicate that the period is imminent, (e.g. pain in the abdomen), must treat *any day* on which similar symptoms occur as a *menstruation date, beside* the usual three *menstruation dates.* (For full details see Page 89.) If such symptoms occur before the day of the period a *sha'aloh* should be asked.

Fluctuation within Three Days

If a woman's cycle fluctuates within a three day limit e.g. she menstruates always between the 27th and 29th day, a *sha'aloh* should be asked as to whether *all* these days need to be kept *as menstruation days* on a regular basis or not.

Fresh Bleeding after a Short Interval

If fresh bleeding occurs after a relatively short interval e.g. after fifteen or eighteen days after the beginning of a period. Rabbinical guidance should be sought how to calculate future *menstruation dates*, since *two* sets of *menstruation dates* will have to be observed in the following month.

	S	M	T	W	Th	F	שבת
Week 1				P1	2	3	4
Week 2	5	6	7	8	9	10	11
Week 3	12	13	14	15	16	17	18
Week 4	19	20	21	22	23	24	25
Week 5	26	27	28 P2 1	2	3	4	5
Week 6	6	7	8	9	10	11	12
Week 7	13	14	15	16	17	18 P3	19
Week 8	20	21	22	23	24	25	26
Week 9	27	28	29	30?(1)	31?(1)		
Week 10		(2)					
Week 11					?(3)		(4)
Week 12	?(5)						

?(1) 30th or 31st day from P2; (2) 18th day from P3; ?(3) 28th day from P3; (4) 30th day from P3; ?(5) 31st day from P3

Summary:

1.   Menstruation dates are calculated on the basis of the previous periods.

2.   All eventualities are covered if one marks the 30th and 31st day *plus* the date which corresponds to the last interval.

3.   If a *regular* pattern, is noticed, rabbinical guidance should be sought.

4.   Women who have definite symptoms before the period starts must treat as menstruation dates also *any* day on which such symptoms occur.

The Menopause

Before the menopause[6] the periods tend to become very irregular, (e.g. there may be one interval of fifty or sixty days and then a number of intervals of less than thirty days). This irregularity may continue for a number of years. Normal marital relations are permitted nevertheless, as long as they observe the usual two or three *menstruation days*, and as long as she is watchful for signs of an oncoming period. (It is advisable, for the sake of one's own peace of mind, to precede marital relations by a *b'dikoh*.)

A woman in her fifties who has a period after an interval of at least ninety days, should establish by a *sha'aloh* whether the usual *menstruation dates* will need to be observed during the following month or not.

---

6. Usually between the age of forty and fifty.

CHAPTER FOURTEEN

SPOTTING

כתמים

A woman may notice occasionally[1] during her *clean* days a stain of blood on her body or on her underwear, or on her bed linen. This is referred to as *spotting* or *staining* (*Ke'sem*), provided that it was *not preceded by any physical symptoms* which alerted her that there may be an issue of blood.

WHAT IS THE *DIN* OF A *KESEM*?

On her Body

If the stain is found on her body or on a sanitary pad a *sha'aloh* is required, even if the stain is very small.

On Underwear

If a stain is noticed on underwear or bed linen it would

---

1. Where spotting occurs frequently, medical advice is recommended.

depend on the size of the stain and on the type of the material and its colour, whether she becomes *niddoh* or not.

Size of Stain

A stain on underwear or bed linen renders a woman *niddoh* only if it covers a minimum area which is equal to the area of a circle with a diameter of 19 mm. If the spot is of uneven shape, a *sha'aloh* should be asked in order to determine its area. If a number of unconnected spots are noticed, each one smaller than the required area, she remains *clean*.

Note: If blood was found on underwear etc. as a result of an obligatory[2] investigation, as in the case where she felt a discharge, she would be *unclean*, however small the area is.

Stains on Coloured Material

Staining renders a woman *unclean* only if it occurred on white or near white material. Stains on a coloured material, are *clean*.

Note: This does not apply to blood found on coloured material as a result of an obligatory investigation, or if blood was noticed on coloured material used for a *b'dikoh*.[3]

A stain on partly white, partly coloured material requires a *sha'aloh*.

Frequent Spotting

Women who experience frequent spotting or who frequently have discharges of a doubtful colour (i.e. discharges which were not felt at the time of the discharge) are advised to

---

2. See Page 53.
3. This would normally not happen, since examinations are made with a white cloth.

use coloured underwear and bed linen - except during the *seven clean days*.

Note: During the first three of the *seven clean days* and on expected *menstruation dates all* spots require a *sha'aloh*.

The following instances require a *sha'aloh*:

a)   If the stain is of doubtful origin and may have originated from another source such as a wound or red dye;

b)   If one is in doubt whether it is blood or not;

c)   If one is in doubt whether the stain was on the garment before it was worn (and originated from a previous period).

d)   If blood was found on: toilet tissue, cotton wool, etc. as a result of wiping; on the lavatory seat; in the bath water or on the floor. If she suffers from haemorrhoids she must not automatically assume that the blood is due to this. A *Rav* must be consulted.

   Note: Some women have the tendency to look at the toilet tissue after wiping. This should be discouraged as this may cause unnecessary *sha'alos*.

e)   If blood was found in urine.[4]

f)   Blood found on her body - however little.

g)   Coloured stains found on undergarments.

---

4. Even if she experiences pain when urinating or if she thinks that she has a wound.

No need to record

If a woman became *niddoh* due to spotting the date need not be recorded.

Note: A woman who notices a *kesem* (stain) need not make a *b'dikoh*, unless her period is imminent.

Summary:

1. Spots of a certain minimum size found on white underwear or bed linen etc., render her a *niddoh*.

2. Blood of doubtful origin requires a *sha'aloh*.

CHAPTER FIFTEEN

CONDUCT DURING UNCLEAN DAYS

During the time a woman is *tomeh* i.e. from the beginning of the *niddoh* period until after *t'viloh*, conduct between husband and wife is subject to certain restrictions which serve as a reminder and as a restraint.[1] In consideration of *tzni'us* these should be done as unobtrusively as possible. However, avoiding embarrassment is not a ground for making exceptions to any of these laws. These restrictions apply in addition to complete abstention from marital relations.

Touching and Passing of Objects

Husband and wife may not touch one another, not even the clothes of the other, even if they protrude. They must not carry

---

1. See Chapter Twelve for conduct on days when the period is anticipated, but has not yet arrived.

an object together and neither pass nor throw anything one to the other, even into the other's lap.

One partner must not pass a baby to the other, play with or kiss, or feed a baby when it is on the other's lap. In a difficult situation one may take a child from the other if the child is old enough "to go by itself". If there is *no other alternative* one would be permitted to take even a younger child from the other but without touching the other.

Sharing a Seat

It is permitted for the husband and wife to share a fixed or very heavy bench which does not shake when one sits on it, provided that they sit slightly apart.

They must not share an ordinary bench or couch, even if they sit some distance apart. Many authorities permit it if a third person sits between them.

Sharing a Bed

Husband and wife must not share one bed, even a double bed with separate mattresses.

Note: No exception can be made to this law — even temporarily, e.g. if they are unable to obtain a hotel room with separate beds.

Their beds must stand a little apart so that even their bedcovers do not touch. If possible the distance should be 60 cm approx. (so that the outstretched hand of one would not touch the bed of the other).

The wife must not lie on her husband's bed when he is present. He must not lie or sit on her bed even if she is *not* present except when she is out of town. They must not use each other's pillows or cushions, but, if they are identical it would not matter if they get exchanged when the beds are made.

Eating Together

When they eat at one table a *reminder* is required for husband and wife to refrain from closer contact. The following are regarded as reminders:

a)   They place on the table *between* them a slightly conspicuous object which is not normally on the table e.g. an extra[2] jug (empty or full), an extra loaf of bread, a vase etc. (Spare cutlery or saucers are not conspicuous enough).

b)   They eat on separate tablecloths, or one of them has an extra table napkin, on which he/she eats.

c)   She does not sit in her usual place.

It is widely accepted that when other people are present, adults or older children, no reminder is required.[3] If possible, however, she should sit a little further away from her husband than usually.

Eating out of one plate

Husband and wife must not eat out of one plate or share the same cup either by drinking from it alternately or by using straws.

If the food is served from a dish on to individual plates it is not considered as eating from one plate and is permitted. If a fruit bowl or cake dish is placed in the centre of the table he and she may take from it.

---

2. Extra - i.e. not for use at that meal.
3. Some require a reminder even then.

Left overs

The wife may eat or drink anything left over by her husband; but he must not eat or drink anything left over by her if she is in the same room[4] unless it is first transferred to another plate or cup. If the husband was not aware that his wife ate or drank from it, there is no need to tell him.

An *empty* cup from which his wife drunk may be used by him (e.g. a cup of a thermos-flask) but it is preferable to rinse it first. If they have only one cup e.g. on a journey, it would be preferable for him to take the first drink.

Serving Food with a Change

When the wife brings food for her husband or serves it out at the table, it is preferable to put it down in a slightly unusual way. For example, she should place it in front of him with her left hand or set it down slightly away from him. This applies also to drinks. But, if she actually prepares the drink in front of him e.g. she puts tea and water etc. into a cup, it may well be obligatory to place it before him after that in an unusual manner.

If a husband brings food or drink for his wife or shares it out at the table, it would be preferable to make a change as above e.g. when he shares out *challoh* after *kiddush*.

When the husband leaves some *kiddush* wine or *kos shel b'rochoh* (after *benshing*) only for his wife (i.e. the wine is not shared by the rest of the family), he should leave his cup on the table and she should take it on her own accord, i.e. he should neither put the cup down in front of her nor transfer it to another cup.

---

4. If he started to eat from the food left over by her while she was out of the room and she then came back, he may continue eating it.

PERSONAL ATTENTION

Making the Bed

The wife must not make her husband's bed in his presence. This includes spreading[5] the sheets or blankets, putting on quilts, duvets or pillows. Straightening the bed merely so that the house looks tidy is permitted. Heavier work connected with preparing the bed e.g. putting up a bed or putting the mattress on the bed, is not considered as personal attention and is permitted. The husband must not make his wife's bed in her presence e.g. if she is not well.

Preparing Water for Washing

The wife must not pour out water for him at the time when he is washing. It is also preferable that she does not prepare water for him in his presence, i.e. bringing him a jug or dish of water or filling his bath. Preparing water for *n'tilas yodayim* is permitted.

The same applies to the husband with regard to his wife, i.e. he must not prepare water for her etc.

ATTENTION DURING ILLNESS

When the Husband is Ill

When the husband is fairly ill and there is no one to nurse him, his wife may attend to him; she may set out food in front of him (and, if necessary, even feed him), she may bring him water, pass him anything he needs, or help him to sit up or even to get

---

5. Or adjusting of sheets, pillows, blankets etc. so that the bed should be ready for use.

dressed. She should avoid, however, if possible, to make his bed in his presence and to wash him.

When the Wife is Ill

When the wife is ill the husband may attend to her, if necessary, in the following manner:

He may bring her meals and set them out before her in the usual way. He may bring her water for washing and, if necessary, pass into her hand anything that she needs e.g. a cup or cutlery. But, he must not wash her (even with a sponge), touch her (even for taking her pulse) or sit her up or make her bed in her presence.

If she is very ill - even if not dangerously - and his assistance is very much needed, all the above restrictions are waived. But taking the pulse and touching her even for medical attention, is permitted only if she is dangerously ill.

If his wife falls and is unable to get up her husband may help her.

A doctor must not examine his own wife unless she is dangerously ill and no other doctor is on call or if he is the better doctor. Even then, he should cover the area he is going to examine with a cloth, if possible.

If a woman needs injections regularly a *sha'aloh* should be asked whether or not her husband may give them to her.

TRAVELLING TOGETHER

Ordinary Travelling

When husband and wife are travelling by motor car on a *non-leisure* trip there are no restrictions as to where they may sit, provided that they ensure not to come into contact even when the car stops suddenly or takes a corner. It is necessary therefore, for them to sit well apart or to place a broad object between them e.g. a shopping bag.

When they travel in a taxi, bus, train or airplane, the main concern should be to sit in a way that they cannot come into contact.[6] On a long journey it is advisable to sit on opposite seats or on seats with a separation between the two seats.

Pleasure Driving

Husband and wife who embark on a pleasure trip in a motor car must sit on separate seats. Many authorities permit the husband and wife to sit on the same seat, as long as a third person sits between them. But it is not sufficient to merely place an object between them.

They must not be together in a rowing or motor boat because of the frequent movement, but a large boat is considered like a motor car.

Conversation

Conversation should be conducted in the usual friendly way but they must refrain from intimate or frivolous talk. (Problems relating to *dinim* of *niddoh* may, of course, be discussed.)

A woman must not neglect her appearance during the time of separation. The husband is permitted to enjoy the beauty of his wife, even when she is *niddoh*, but he must not look at her (at this time) while she is not properly dressed[7] or when her hair is

---

6. So that they will not collide when the car takes a sharp corner or stops suddenly.

7. e.g. When she is breast feeding, or getting dressed or undressed, or when she is getting washed.

uncovered. He may not listen to her singing or purposely smell the perfume which she is wearing.

Summary:

Husband and wife must observe certain restrictions during the *niddoh* period regarding: physical contact, eating together, serving food, sharing the same seat and personal attention.

CHAPTER SIXTEEN

LAWS FOR A BRIDE

Fixing the Wedding Date

When fixing the wedding day,[1] care must be taken to calculate that the wedding and the first few days after the wedding take place during a 'safe' time i.e. not during the time the oncoming period is anticipated and not within the first fifteen days after a period. The ideal time would be, in the majority of cases, near the beginning of the fourth week after a period. To make this calculation possible it is necessary to keep an account of the previous three or four periods.

	S	M	T	W	T	F	ש	
Week 1			P					← usual unsuitable time
Week 2								
Week 3								← usual safe time
Week 4				*	*	*	*	← *suggested wedding days
Week 5								← usual unsafe time

---

1. These calculations can be made only by an experienced person.

Preparing for the Wedding

All brides, including widows, and even women past their menopause must undergo the full[2] *ta'haroh* process of counting seven days and *t'viloh* before their wedding because the excitement of getting married is a cause for a possible show of blood.

The bride commences the *ta'haroh* preparations about ten days before her wedding to enable her to go to *t'viloh* not later than the night before her wedding[3] or, the latest on the wedding day itself. (See next Chapter for the *dinim* of a bride who is still *niddoh*.)

Special Rulings for a Bride

A bride may make her *hef'sek ta'haroh* even before the fifth day and start counting if the *hef'sek ta'haroh* was satisfactory.

A bride may go to *t'viloh* during daytime, (after the seventh day). If the seventh[4] day falls on the day of the wedding and the *chupoh* will take place after nightfall she may go to *t'viloh* even during daytime of the seventh day.

Examinations after *T'viloh*

If *t'viloh* takes place a number of days before the wedding, one *b'dikoh* per day is required, on the days following the *t'viloh*, as an extra precaution, up to and including the day of the wedding.

---

2. See Chapters Four to Seven.
3. But not earlier than four days before her wedding.
4. Of the *seven clean days*.

CHAPTER SEVENTEEN

AFTER THE WEDDING

Bride who is *Niddoh*

If the bride is *niddoh* at the time of the *chupoh* the bridegroom must be informed. A *Rav* should be consulted concerning the special laws which apply in such circumstances, both during and after the *chupoh*. The primary concern is that the couple must not be together on their own even during daytime until after *t'viloh*. No concession can be made regarding touching one another e.g. holding hands when going away from the *chupoh* or at a *mitzvoh*-dance, although this may cause embarrassment.

The First Night[1]

There is a possibility and likelihood of slight bleeding as a result of the first marital act of a virgin. Husband and wife must

---

1. *Seforim* e.g. *Siddur* must not lie uncovered in a room when intercourse takes place. They require a double cover. The room should be dark.

separate,[2] therefore, *after* its conclusion, as if she were a *niddoh*, *even if no blood was noticed.* (This does not apply in the case where the bride was a widow or a divorcee.)

If there was no possibility of bleeding on account of incomplete[3] marital contact, separation is not necessary, but first she must examine herself and the sheet on which she was lying to see that there is no trace of blood. If he is not sure and she also does not know, a *sha'aloh* is required. They should separate for the moment. Separation will be necessary after the *next* successful marital act.

The First *Ta'haroh* Procedure

If there is sufficient time to follow the *ta'haroh* procedure before the next period is due, i.e. at least twelve[4] days, she may count - on this occasion,[5] as an exception - only four days, and then make the *hef'sek ta'haroh* examination of on the fourth day. If successful, she counts her *seven clean days* and goes to *t'viloh* at nightfall following the last day of the *seven clean days.*

Example: If the wedding took place on Sunday, and they had to separate on that night, then the *hef'sek ta'haroh* can be made on Thursday, and the subsequent *t'viloh* will take place the following Thursday night.

If there is insufficient time for the full *ta'haroh* procedure before the next period is due, then separation has to be

---

2. See Chapter Fifteen. Although the virginal blood does not originate from the womb, she is to be considered like a *niddoh*.

3. i.e. there was *no* penetration or only the penetration of the tip (or even if *he is in doubt* whether the penetration was a little deeper - but *he is certain* that there was no full penetration).

4. If the next period is anticipated *on* the twelfth day a *sha'aloh* should be asked.

5. Because, in this instance, the blood did not originate from the womb and he status of *tum'oh* is *miderabonon*.

maintained until *t'viloh* will take place, after the following period. In this case the *hef'sek ta'haroh* examination may take place as soon as the bleeding stops, even on the third or fourth day (as there were already a total of five days of compulsory separation).

The First *T'viloh* Night After the Wedding

If blood is noticed also after marital relations of the first *t'viloh* night after the wedding or if the first complete marital act occurred only on this occasion, separation is required. The same routine is followed as after the wedding night.[6] This procedure must be continued until a *t'viloh*-night passes without evidence of blood. (See Page 89)

Note: If normal marital relations passed with no evidence of blood, and after that blood was again noticed after marital relations, an urgent *sha'aloh* must be asked as to whether this blood can still be attributed to virginal blood.

Normal Marital Relations

After the initial separation(s) normal marital relations are permitted[7] on any day she is not *niddoh* except on *menstruation days* (see Chapter Twelve), *Yom Kippur, Ninth of Av,*[8] and when either the husband or his wife is sitting *shiv'oh*[9] ח״ו.

For conduct of the husband and his wife see Part Two Chapter Two.

---

6. i.e. she can make a *hef'sek ta'haroh* after four days, wait the seven days and after that go to *mikveh*.

7. Marital relations are not to take place during the day or if there is light in the room or in the open, even in the night, or if there are *seforim* which are not covered (with a double cover).

8. Even when *Tish'oh B'Av* falls on *Shabbos*.

9 .Seven days of mourning.

Examination Before and After Marital Relations

It should be established early in the marriage whether she is inclined to bleeding from the *womb* due to marital relations. (This is a very rare yet serious phenomenon). This would not happen to a woman who has a regular period, or to a woman with an irregular period during her 'safe' days i.e. the time when she normally never menstruates. Example: A woman whose interval between periods fluctuates between 24 and 29 days is said to be 'safe' up to the 24th day.

The Examination

A total of three sets of examinations are required. On the first three occasions when marital relations take place *after* the safe days,[10] circumstances permitting, an examination is to be made by her beforehand[11] and *immediately afterwards* to check whether there was an issue of blood or not. Mostly there *will not be* any blood. The husband needs to examine himself also. If there were three clear results no further examinations will be necessary.

Summary:

Separation is usually necessary after the wedding night, and sometimes also after the next few occasions of marital relations.

Three examinations are required early in marriage to establish that periods are not brought on by marital relations.

෴ॐ෴

---

10. Marital relations cannot take place very often after the safe days. It may therefore take a long time before they manage the three examinations, sometimes it may even take a number of years.
11. The purpose of the examination beforehand is to establish that she was clear before the marital relations.

CHAPTER EIGHTEEN

PREGNANCY AND CHILDBIRTH

During Pregnancy

Menstruation dates[1] must be observed in the first month of pregnancy although the cycle of periods normally ceases, but women with a regular period must continue to observe their usual *menstruation dates*[2] during the first three months of pregnancy.

If bleeding occurs during pregnancy due to a threatened miscarriage or any other cause the woman becomes a *niddoh*. *Menstruation dates* will need to be observed in the following month in the usual way. See Chapters Twelve and Thirteen.

---

1. See Chapters Twelve and Thirteeen.
2. i.e. if she had a regular lunar cycle (See Page 86).

Childbirth[3]

A woman who is in an advanced stage of labour is considered a *niddoh* even if no show of blood had occurred. If her waters break she is also a *niddoh*. In a case where labour pains began but later stopped a *sha'aloh* is necessary.

After Childbirth

A woman remains *niddoh* after childbirth, until she counts the *seven clean days* and goes to *t'viloh*.

The counting may begin in theory as soon as she is clear[4] (provided that *t'viloh* takes place after the fifteenth day). In practice many factors have to be considered as to how long she should wait after childbirth before she goes to *t'viloh*. (See Page 51)

Women may find it useful to revise the laws of counting and preparing for *t'viloh* etc. after childbirth, as these were not practiced for many months.

After a Miscarriage

A woman who has a miscarriage becomes a *niddoh*. *T'viloh* must not take place until after the fifteenth day (inclusive of the *seven clean days*).

First Two Years After Childbirth

The usual cycle of periods ceases for a number of months after childbirth. For that, the onset of an oncoming period need not be anticipated after childbirth and *menstruation dates* need

---

3. See "Childbirth on *Shabbos* and *Yom Tov*" by the same author.
4. But not before five days after the birth.

not be observed until the first period occurs. After that the usual *menstruation dates* must be observed.

A woman who had a *regular* period before her pregnancy, need not anticipate the re-establishment of that cycle until two years after the birth of the child.

CHAPTER NINETEEN

THE IRREGULAR PERIOD

וסת שאינו קבוע

Definition

A woman whose periods follow no regular pattern is said to have an irregular period.

Menstruation Days

We explained in Chapter Twelve that precautionary separation is necessary on the day the oncoming period is anticipated. A woman who has an irregular period cannot know the *exact* day on which to expect the period. She must take into consideration, therefore, *all* common cycles as possible menstruation days and keep the relevant *dinim* on each of them.

These are the three common cycles:-

1.   The lunar cycle - וסת החדש

2.   The 'same-interval' cycle - וסת הפלגה

3.   The 'thirty days' or 'average' cycle - עונה בינונית

(Compare Chapter Thirteen - Page 60)

1.   The Lunar Cycle

According to the lunar cycle, the period recurs on *the same date* of the current Jewish month as in the last month irrespective of whether the preceding month had 29 or 30 days.[1] The calculations can be made only with the aid of a Jewish calendar.

Example: If the date of the last period was the 3rd of *Cheshvan* one marks the 3rd of *Kislev* as the expected *menstruation date* irrespective of whether *Cheshvan* has 29 or 30 days.

2.   The 'Same-interval' Cycle

According to the 'same-interval' cycle, the period recurs after an interval which corresponds to the interval between the last two periods. In the calculations one counts both days inclusive.

Example: Period A occurred on Wednesday and Period B 28 days after that, i.e. on Tuesday of the fourth week. One marks as a possible menstruation day the 28th day following that Tuesday i.e. the Monday of the fourth week. (See Page 60 for the calculation of the intervals and the diagrams on Pages 59 and 61)

---

1. It is important to be aware that the length of the Jewish months fluctuate between 29 and 30 days. *The last day* of a month with 30 days is called 'the first day of *Rosh Chodesh*', although, in fact, only the next day is the first day of the next month, i.e. the second day *Rosh Chodesh*.

3. The 'Thirty Days' Cycle

According to the 'thirty days' cycle, the period recurs on the 30th day (both days inclusive). Call the day the pervious period began day one and mark the 30th day as a possible *menstruation day*. (Some *poskim* are of the opinion that this 30th day is calculated from the day *following* the period i.e. the 31st day following the last period (both days inclusive).

Lunar Cycle and 'Thirty Days' Cycle Coinciding

If the Jewish month during which the last period occurred had 29 days, then the *menstruation dates* according to the lunar cycle and the 'thirty days' cycle will coincide.

Based on Last Period

Menstruation dates for the irregular period are calculated on the basis of the last period only. All previous dates and previous intervals are ignored.[2]

Example[3] for calculating the three menstruation dates:

Period P2 occurred on the 3rd *Nissan* after an interval of 26[4] days. Three dates are marked as *menstruation dates* (see Chart A):-

1.   28th *Nissan* - in consideration of the interval of 26 days between P1 and P2.

---

2. Some conduct themselves according to a more stringent view in so far that this applies only if the *previous* interval was *shorter* than the very last interval and was thus canceled, but if the previous interval was longer, both intervals are taken into consideration.
3. See also Pages 59 - 61.
4. Both days inclusive.

2. 2nd *Iyar*, the 30th day after P2 - in consideration of the 'thirty days' cycle.

3. 3rd *Iyar* which corresponds to the 3rd *Nissan* - in consideration of the lunar cycle.

If period P3 occurred on the 1st *Iyar* - an interval of 29 days - one marks the following days as possible *menstruation dates*. (see Chart B):-

1. 29th *Iyar* - in consideration of the interval of 29 days between P2 and P3.

2. 1st *Sivan* - in consideration of the lunar cycle and the 'thirty-day' cycle which coincide in this case as the period occurred in a month of 29 days. (According to the opinion that the 'thirty-day' cycle is counted from the day following the period, one marks also the 2nd *Sivan* (see Page 87 - The thirty days cycle).

CHART A

	S	M	T	W	Th	F	שבת
Week 1						1 P1	2
Week 2	3	4	5	6	7	8	9
Week 3	10	11	12	13	14	15	16
Week 4	17	18	19	20	21	22	23
5	24 1st ניסן	25	26 P2 1 3rd ניסן	2	3	4	5
Week 6	6	7	8	9	10	11	12
Week 7	13	14	15	16	17	18	19
Week 8	20	21	22	23	24	25	26 28th סיון
Week 9	27	28	29 1st אייר	30	31 3rd אייר		

CHART B

	S	M	T	W	Th	F	שבת
Week 1						1 P1	2
Week 2	3	4	5	6	7	8	9
Week 3	10	11	12	13	14	15	16
Week 4	17	18	19	20	21	22	23
Week 5	24 1st ניסן	25	26 P2 1 3rd ניסן	2	3	4	5
Week 6	6	7	8	9	10	11	12
Week 7	13	14	15	16	17	18	19
Week 8	20	21	22	23	24	25	26
Week 9	27	28	29 P3 1 1st אייר	2	3	4	5
Week 10	6	7	8	9	10	11	12
Week 11	13	14	15	16	17	18	19
Week 12	20	21	22	23	24	25	26
Week 13	27	28	29 29th אייר	30 1st סיון	31 2nd סיון		

Physical Symptoms (וסת הגוף)

If a woman experiences[5] definite physical symptoms shortly before her period commences, in addition to the usual pre-menstrual discomfort, she is considered as having a 'symptom-cycle'. If similar symptoms would occur after that on *any* date, she must treat *that* day as a *menstruation date in addition* to her usual three *menstruation dates* (see Page 85). If the *same type* of

---

5. See Page 61 "period preceded by symptoms".

symptoms recur three times, she will have established a *Regular Physical Symptom Cycle*.

The following are common symptoms: - Repeated yawning, hiccuping, sneezing, griping, an urge to stretch one's hands, feeling of pain at the centre or lower part of the abdomen, heat flushes or temperature, headaches, heaviness in bones, a clean discharge preceding the period.

Summary:

1.   In the case of the irregular period three cycles must be taken into consideration as possible *menstruation dates*.

2.   When calculating *menstruation dates* of the irregular period one needs to consider only the date of the *last* period and the interval between the last two periods. For laws of conduct on *menstruation dates* see Chapter Twelve Page 56.

3.   If physical symptoms precede the period *on* the day the period occurred, these must be considered in future as a possible signal of an oncoming period.

CHAPTER TWENTY

THE REGULAR PERIOD

וסת קבוע

Definition

A woman is said to have a regular period if three consecutive periods follow a regular pattern. Three regular periods are sufficient to establish a *lunar cycle*, but for the *same-interval cycle* three equal *intervals* are required i.e. a total of four periods.

Time of Day

A regular period is established only if each of the periods started at the same time i.e. either in daytime between sunrise and sunset, or at night between sunset and sunrise.

Changing from Irregular to Regular

A woman who usually has an irregular period may develop a regular pattern, even if only for a limited[1] time. It is necessary, therefore, to keep the last three periods always under surveillance in case a regularity develops.

Recognizing a Regular Period

Periods occurring in one of the following sequences are considered regular:-

a) *Regular lunar-cycle.* Three consecutive periods on the same date of the Jewish month.

b) *Regular-interval cycle.* Three equal intervals between period days, counted from beginning to beginning of period.

c) *Regular same-day cycle.* Three consecutive periods on the same day of the week with equal intervals between period days e.g. every 4th Wednesday.

d) *Regular physical-symptoms cycle.* Three consecutive periods preceded by definite physical symptoms.

e) *Regular physical-cause cycle.* Three consecutive periods caused by a physical experience.

f) *Regular changing-dates cycle.* A sequence of periods following a regular pattern on changing dates, e.g. 2nd, 3rd, 4th of consecutive months and then again 2nd, 3rd, 4th of consecutive months, and a third time 2nd, 3rd, 4th of consecutive months.

---

1. Permanent regular periods are very rare nowadays except 'the same day cycle' and 'the physical symptoms cycle'. These sections should be read with particular care. See c and d.

g)   *Regular changing-interval cycle.* A sequence of periods
       following a regular pattern with changing intervals e.g.
       intervals of 27-28-29 days; 27-28-29 days; 27-28-29 days.

Physical-symptoms Cycle (d)

A physical symptoms cycle is established if on three
consecutive occasions the period was preceded, *on the day of the
period* by definite symptoms besides the usual pre-menstrual
discomfort e.g. pain in the lower or central part of the abdomen,
repeated yawning, etc. (for further symptoms see Page 61).

If the symptoms occur on irregular days it is a *simple*
physical-symptoms cycle. If they occur on regular days on the
lines of cycles (a), (b), (c), (f), (g), it is a *regular physical cycle.*

In the case of the simple physical-symptoms cycle, there is
no fixed date on which the period is to be expected. The onset of
the period is to be suspected on any day on which the symptoms
occur.

If there is a *regular physical symptoms cycle*, menstruation
dates depend on the coinciding of both, i.e. the symptoms
appearing *on the regular date.* If no symptoms develop on the
regular date, or if the symptoms appear on another day, the
period need not be expected, once a regular period is established.

Physical Cause Cycle (e)

In rare cases a period may be brought on by physical strain
e.g. jumping, bending, or eating extremely sharp or highly-
seasoned food. If the period started on three consecutive
occasions, on the day the physical cause took place, or on the
following day a *physical-cause cycle* is established. There exist
simple and combined *physical-cause cycles.* (Compare *physical-
symptoms cycle.*)

Menstruation Dates During Regular Periods

As long as a regular period continues without even temporary variations, her regular cycle *menstruation date* only needs to be considered. If a change occurs, *even once*, three *menstruation dates* must be taken into consideration in the following month:

1.   her own regular cycle,

2.   the new date of the Jewish month,

3.   the new interval (but not the 30th day cycle).

The reason for this is that we must suspect that she may change to a new pattern. If the next period recurs again on her regular period date, the changed date is cancelled and the regular date only needs to be kept in future.

Note: It is common for a woman with a regular period to experience continuously changes from her regular pattern. She may change once, or twice to a new pattern, but then go back to her regular pattern once or twice and then again change. In such a case her regular cycle would still be upheld. This undetermined state may continue for a very long time, yet every time a change occurs she must keep the *three menstruation dates* stated above.

Missing a Period

If a woman with a *regular-interval cycle*, misses her period for one month, her previous interval need not be taken into consideration until the onset of the next period. She then needs to consider:

1.   her usual interval,

2.   the new interval (which may be approximately double than her usual period),

3.   the new Jewish date.

In the case of the *lunar-cycle*, however, the usual *menstruation date is* upheld although she missed her period for one month.

Change From One Regular Period To Another

If a change occurs in three consecutive months on the lines of a new regular pattern, a new regular period is established. The previous pattern is cancelled for good, unless it reoccurs *three* times.

Change from Regular to Irregular Period

If a change occurs in three consecutive months, on the lines of an *irregular* pattern, her regular period is cancelled. If, however, the dates of the original *regular* period return even once, even after a long time (even after a number of years!), the regular cycle is immediately re-established with all its implications, and a further three changes would be required to cancel it.

Verifying a Change

If it appears to a woman with a regular period that she did not menstruate on her regular day, verification is required by an examination[2] on the next day to ascertain that in fact no bleeding occurred on that day. If no examination took place it cannot be accepted as a change in relation to the existing pattern, i.e. she must suspect that bleeding may have taken place on her usual day. A *Rav* should be consulted for future calculations.

---

2. This examination is obligatory in any case (see Page 56).

SUMMARY OF DIFFERENCES BETWEEN REGULAR AND IRREGULAR PERIODS

Regular Period

1. Only one - the regular - *menstruation date* must be kept, unless a change occurs.

2. If a change occurs, the regular cycle *and* the new date and interval must be considered for the time being until three consecutive changes occur and the regular period is cancelled.

3. If the examination on the menstruation day was omitted she is considered a *niddoh*, unless an examination with clean results took place after that day (see Page 58).

4. A woman who *always* maintains a regular period, need not do "the three examinations" before and after marital relations (see Page 81).

Irregular Period

1. Two of three menstruation dates must be kept.

2. Menstruation dates are calculated on the basis of the last period only.

3. If the examination on the menstruation days was omitted, she is nevertheless assumed to be *clean*, but *the 30th day* is treated in this respect like a regular period day and she must examine herself on the next day (see Page 57).

4. Early in marriage, examinations before and after marital relations are necessary on three occasions when marital relations take place at a 'non-safe' time (see Page 81).

CHAPTER TWENTY ONE

MORE ABOUT KEDUSHOH

Relationship with Other Couples

Socializing with other people is important but only men with men and women with women. Married people must not think that being married is an automatic shield against outside attractions.[נו] It is not!

It is due probably to this fallacy that it has become fashionable for young couples to socialise with their friends with regular visits and return visits. This gives rise to a situation where one is on first-name relationships with the other couple. Such relationships are counter-productive and can have a devastating effect on a happy marriage. When friendly couples relax in armchairs, engage in light talk and join in a coffee or a *le'chayim* they expose themselves to be seen and they also cannot avoid to see more than they should see.[נו] It would be quite inhuman if this were not to lead to drawing comparisons between their friend's and their own spouse. Such meetings also have the effect of breaking a woman's *tzni'us*. For inevitably she will try to create a good impression on her friend's husband and, probably, her husband will also expect this of her so that he should not be shown up as not having a smart wife.

Young couples are well advised not to undermine their marriage-edifice on account of social pressures and to retain high standards of *kedushoh* and *tzni'us*.

CHAPTER TWENTY TWO

אמירה לבית יעקב

EXTRACTS FROM AN ADDRESS OF RABBENU YONAH TO WOMEN

Chinuch

When the *Torah* was given *Moshe Rabbenu* addressed the women first. Why? Because it would be *their* function to see that their young children learn *Torah* by attending regularly a *Cheder* or a *Talmud Torah*. It would be the sweet and loving voice of the mother, her tender and encouraging words, her warmth and the light in her face which would endear *Torah* to the children and infuse them with a permanent love for learning *Torah*. The importance of this gentle approach cannot be over emphasised because a stable *Torah* life is the result of a pleasant *Torah* atmosphere in childhood.

Hand in hand with instilling the love of *Torah* to her child it is also the privilege of the mother to imbue him with *yir'as shomayim*. If a mother takes this task seriously, the credit of all future *Torah* and *Yir'oh* of her child will go to the mother.

Such mothers are the backbone of *Torah* in *Yisroel*.

T'filloh

A woman should endeavour to *daven* daily, if possible, three times a day. At the end of *Sh'moneh Essreh* (before *osseh sholom*) she should pour out her heart in prayer to *Hashem Yisborach* (in whichever language she prefers), especially during the time when she is pregnant, that her children should be G-d fearing and that her sons should be successful in their *Torah* learning. For, the ultimate reward and eternal happiness of a mother is if her children go in the *derech Hashem*. When she will be in *olom haboh* the *mitzvos* of her children will be accredited to her as if she herself is performing them.

Shabbos Lights

Women should take care to be ready in good time for *Shabbos* and light the *Shabbos* candles early. This is an opportune time to *daven* for the success of her children in *Torah* learning and that they should have the merit to fulfill many *mitzvos*.

This is a suggested text for her *t'filloh*:

יְהִי רָצוֹן שֶׁיִּהְיוּ בָּנַי מְאִירִים בָּעוֹלָם בַּתּוֹרָה וּבְמִצְווֹת וּבְיִרְאַת שָׁמַיִם

During pregnancy she should also pray:

יְהִי רָצוֹן שֶׁיְּהֵא הַוָּלָד יְרֵא שָׁמַיִם וְחָכָם וּמַצְלִיחַ בַּתּוֹרָה וּבְמִצְווֹת

To Support her Husband in *Torah* Learning

When her husband comes home tired and fatigued from work it is often difficult for him to take the initiative to study *Torah*.

A wife who understands the importance of learning *Torah* and its immeasurable merit will look for ways how to encourage and motivate him even at a time when it is difficult for him. This can be done only in a loving and non-domineering manner. It must be done without pushing or nagging, but rather by expressing how happy *she* would be if he would learn for a while as this means so much to her.

Sholom Bayis

True *sholom bayis* can be established and maintained only if love permeates their union. The wife's contribution is to speak to her husband in a pleasant tone and to be willing to go out of her way to please him.

Tzni'us

Tzni'us is important in the house but even more important is a high level of *tzni'us* outside the house.

The mother's *tzni'us* determines the level of purity of the child.

HEBREW FOOTNOTES

and

תפלה לבנים ולהצלחתם

 י)   ראה רמב"ן הוזכר בציון 6) וכלשונו שם שמכנה לאיש כזה כמנובל ברשות התורה.

יא)   כמה שמבואר ברמב"ם הל' דעות הנ"ל ציון 6).

CHAPTER THREE

יב)   דבשניהם יש כרת רק דבע"ז וניאוף בעדים יש חיוב מיתה בידי ב"ד.

יג)   דאיסור נדה בכלל פרשת עריות (ויקרא י"ח,י"ט) וכולם הוקשו זו לזו (יבמות ח.) וע' לשון הרמב"ם פי"ד מהל' איסורי ביאה הל' א'. ועל ע"ז שפיכות דמים וגלוי עריות חייב אדם למסור נפשו כמבואר בשולחן ערוך יורה דעה סי' קנ"ז סעי' א'. ואיסור נדה בכלל כמבואר ביו"ד סי' קצ"ה בש"ך ס"ק כ'. ואפילו על מגע ערוה יש דעות שמחויב למסור נפשו עיי"ש ועיין בפ"ת יו"ד סי' קנ"ז ס"ק י"א.

יד)   רמ"א יו"ד סי' קנ"ז סעי' א'.

CHAPTER TWENTY-ONE

טו)   ע"פ גמרא דסוכה דף נ"ב. וז"ל וספדה הארץ משפחות משפחות לבד משפחות בית דוד לבד ונשיהם לבד (זכריה י"ב) אמרו והלא דברים ק"ו ומה לעתיד לבא שעוסקים בהספד (על משיח בן יוסף שיהרג) ואין יצר הרע שולט בהם (בשעת צער) אמרה תורה אנשים לבד ונשים לבד עכשיו שעוסקים בשמחה (של שמחת בית השואבה) על אחת כמה וכמה. ובפרקי אבות נאמר על תרבה שיחה עם האשה. באשתך אמרו ק"ו באשת חברך (אבות פ"א,ה').

טז)   וגם אמרו שחוק וקלות ראש מרגילים את האדם לערוה (פרקי אבות פ"ג,י"ג).

מקורות
לפרקים - ב׳, ג׳ וכ״א

FOOTNOTES
TO CHAPTERS TWO, THREE AND TWENTY-ONE

CHAPTER TWO

א) רש״י ויקרא ט׳, ב׳.

ב) שם.

ג) במדבר ו׳ באבן עזרא ח׳. ואמרינן במס׳ תענית י״א. ״כל היושב בתענית נקרא קדוש״. וע׳ רבינו בחיי במדבר ו׳,ג׳ במה שפירש לשון ״כי נזר״.

ד) ע׳ רמב״ם פ״א דאישות הל׳ א׳ וב׳ דליקוחי הקידושין מצוות עשה מן התורה וכמו שאומרין בברכת הנישואין ״המקדש את עמו ישראל על ידי חופה וקידושין״. ודעת הרמב״ם שהבא על אשה לשם זנות עובר בלאו של לא תהיה קדשה כמבואר בפ״א דאישות הל׳ ד׳.

ואיסור דרך השחתה הוזכר בפסוק במיתת ער ואונן ע׳ רש״י בראשית ל״ח,ט׳ ורש״י ז׳.

ה) דהרי כתיב ״ולא תתורו אחרי לבבכם ואחרי עיניכם״ (במדבר ט״ו,ל״ט).

ו) רמב״ן בריש פרשת קדושים (ויקרא י״ט,ב׳) ורמב״ם הל׳ דעות פ״ה הל׳ ד׳ וה׳.

ז) כדאמרינן ביבמות סוף ס״ג. ״דייני שמצילות אותנו מן החטא״ והבעל משמר את אשתו כדאמרינן בפסחים דף קי״ג. ״בתך בגרה שחרר עבדך ותן לה״.

ח) דברים כ״ד,ה׳.

ט) חינוך מצוה תקפ״ב וראה שם את לשונו הזהב.

לָהֶם בְּלִי נֶדֶר, וּלְהַשִּׂיאָם עִם זוּוּגָם בִּימֵי הַנְּעוּרִים
בְּנַחַת וּבְרֶוַח וּבְשִׂמְחָה. וּמֵהֶם יֵצְאוּ פֵּרוֹת טוֹבוֹת
וּבָנִים צַדִּיקִים זוֹכִים וּמְזַכִּים לְכָל יִשְׂרָאֵל.

וְלֹא יִתְחַלֵּל שִׁמְךָ הַגָּדוֹל עַל יָדֵינוּ וְלֹא עַל יְדֵי
זַרְעֵינוּ חַס וְשָׁלוֹם. וּמַלֵּא כָּל מִשְׁאֲלוֹת לִבֵּנוּ
לְטוֹבָה בִּבְרִיאוּת בְּהַצְלָחָה וְכָל טוֹב. וְיִתְגַּדֵּל כְּבוֹד
שִׁמְךָ הַגָּדוֹל וּכְבוֹד תּוֹרָתֶךָ עַל יָדֵינוּ וְעַל יְדֵי זַרְעֵינוּ
וְזֶרַע זַרְעֵינוּ וְזֶרַע זַרְעֵינוּ תָּמִיד. אָמֵן כֵּן יְהִי רָצוֹן.
יִהְיוּ לְרָצוֹן אִמְרֵי פִי וְהֶגְיוֹן לִבִּי לְפָנֶיךָ ה׳ צוּרִי
וְגוֹאֲלִי.

תפלה לבנים ולהצלחתם

תפלת האבות על בנים מספר קדמון (מתוך סידור ישועות ישראל)

רִבּוֹנוֹ שֶׁל עוֹלָם זַכֵּנוּ (לְהוֹלִיד בָּנִים טוֹבִים מְאִירִים בַּתּוֹרָה וְ)שֶׁיִּהְיוּ בָּנֵינוּ מְאִירִים בַּתּוֹרָה וְיִהְיוּ בְּרִיאִים בְּגוּפָם וְשִׂכְלָם בַּעֲלֵי מִדּוֹת טוֹבוֹת, עוֹסְקִים בַּתּוֹרָה לִשְׁמָהּ. וְתֵן לָהֶם חַיִּים אֲרוּכִים וְטוֹבִים, וְיִהְיוּ מְמוּלָּאִים בַּתּוֹרָה וּבְחָכְמָה וּבְיִרְאַת שָׁמַיִם, וְיִהְיוּ אֲהוּבִים לְמַעֲלָה וְנֶחֱמָדִים לְמַטָּה. וְתַצִּילֵם מֵעַיִן הָרָע וּמִיֵּצֶר הָרָע וּמִכָּל מִינֵי פּוּרְעָנִיּוֹת. וְיִהְיוּ לָהֶם חוּשִׁים בְּרִיאִים לַעֲבוֹדָתֶךָ. וְזַכֵּנִי בְּרַחֲמֶיךָ הָרַבִּים וְאֶת אִשְׁתִּי/וְאֶת בַּעֲלִי שֶׁתְּמַלֵּא מִסְפַּר יָמֵינוּ עַד מְלֹאת שִׁבְעִים שָׁנָה וְיוֹתֵר בְּטוֹב וּבַנְּעִימִים וְאַהֲבָה וְשָׁלוֹם. וְנִזְכֶּה לְגַדֵּל כָּל אֶחָד מִבָּנַי וְכָל אַחַת מִבְּנוֹתַי לַתּוֹרָה וּלְחֻפָּה וּלְמַעֲשִׂים טוֹבִים.

וְתַזְמִין לְכָל אֶחָד מִבָּנַי אֶת בַּת זִוּוּגוֹ וּלְכָל אַחַת מִבְּנוֹתַי אֶת בֶּן זִוּוּגָהּ וְלֹא יוֹדְחוּ לִפְנֵי אֲחֵרִים חַס וְשָׁלוֹם. וּבָרֵךְ מַעֲשֵׂה יָדֵינוּ לִתֵּן לָהֶם מוֹהַר וּמַתָּן בְּעַיִן יָפָה, וְנוּכַל לְקַיֵּם מַה שֶׁאָנוּ מַבְטִיחִים לִתֵּן

מקורות וכו'

לפרקים - ב', ג', י', י"ח, י"ט וכ"ג

תפלה לבנים ולהצלחתם

PART II

THE JEWISH MARRIAGE
AND
SHOLOM BAYIS

CHAPTER ONE

THE JEWISH
MARRIAGE

The *Torah* and the *Kesuboh* document set the boundaries of the obligations of a husband to his wife. He has to support her, clothe her and satisfy her physical needs (*oinoh*).[1] But, just as he has obligations towards her so she has obligations towards him which are an integral part of the marriage contract.[2] We shall discuss briefly their principal obligations in this chapter.

The Husband's Obligations

The husband has to provide food, clothing and all her medical and personal needs.[3] This must be to a standard of at least as high as she was used to before her marriage. If his family has a higher living standard he must provide the higher standard.[4]

The financial obligations towards his wife are stronger than those he has towards his children. If he cannot provide enough for her and for the children, *she would come first.*[5] A

wife who agreed to a lower standard of living prior to her
marriage in view of getting married to a *learner* (someone
who joins a *kolel*) cannot insist at a later stage on her usual
standard.[6] Such matters are best solved in a mutual way by
each one showing a *full* understanding of the circumstances
and needs of the other.

The physical needs of a wife in marriage are protected
by the *Torah* as the verse says: *He must not fail to honour
(lit. diminish) her fixed times.* (See page 122)

The Wife's Obligations

The obligations of a wife include: running of the house,
preparing and serving the meals to her husband and joining
him for the meals as often as is practical.[7]

The *chachomim* enacted that all earnings of a wife
belong to her husband because the husband has to provide for
his wife.[8] This applies even in a case where her income is
larger than his income and even if she is the sole
breadwinner.[9]

The husband cannot insist that his wife must go out to
work. She is obliged to work only if she can work in the
house.[10] It seems unlikely that she would have to train for a
profession in order to be able to work in the house.[11]

If the wife elects to go out to work, with the approval
of her husband, her earnings would go to him, nevertheless.[12]

We are stating the actual halocho here. In practice, such
matters are worked out mutually between husband and wife in
a way that ensures the happiness and satisfaction of both
parties, provided that it is within the framework of *halocho*.

The husband is duty bound to honour the times normally
designated for his wife (*oinoh*) [see page 122]. Her duties in
this area are equally binding even if this would prove
inconvenient at times, except if she is unwell.

Money Brought into the Marriage[13]

It is a fallacy that all that belongs to a wife belongs automatically to her husband. This is not so. The husband has no right to spend her money (except her earnings) either for living or for other expenses without her full agreement. Similarly, neither the husband nor his wife is allowed to sell her property (real estate) or any of her investments with the purpose of using the money for living expenses. According to the *halocho* all property or money etc. which a wife brings into the marriage (i.e. money which she earned beforehand or which was given to her by her father or others) continues to be her's, but her husband is entitled to the profits or the potential income. Example: the rent of property, the income from interest or shares etc. goes to the husband. If shares or a property rise in value and he sells at a profit, this would not be considered as his profit but as her capital gain. He would have to reinvest the full return and the future higher *profits* would go to him.

Presents Given to a Wife by Other Parties

Any presents which are given to a wife unconditionally belong to her basically, but, where appropriate, the husband reaps the *profits* or the potential income. In other words, presents are treated in the same way as any other property belonging to a wife.

A donor who wants to ensure when he gives a present to a married woman that the recipient will have the *full* benefit of his gift or the *full* say on how the gift should be spent, must say so **before** he gives the gift. He should say to her: "This is given only for *your* personal use or for this specific purpose or for what *you* will decide how the money should be spent, **but it is not for your husband.**"

Management of Money

Chazal advised that in matters concerning the house the husband should consult his wife and consider her opinion.[14] If her requests go beyond their means it will not be prudent to comply with them especially at a time when money is short and bills need to be paid. Borrowing money is never the answer, because great care must be taken not to fall into debt.

It is obvious that the husband has the sole right to decide how to spend his earnings and any money belonging to him on the basis of the marriage contract. The wife is not allowed to spend any of his money on her own accord *even for charity* except for small amounts to which her husband would definitely agree. As far as housekeeping money which the husband gives to his wife is concerned, wisdom dictates that he should give her full freedom on how to spend it.

It is well known that no two people think alike. Therefore, if one side is unable to convince the other, **someone** must give way. Rights exist but must not be abused. *Sholom* never prevails if each one insists on his/her rights. On the other hand, if each party will try to understand the *other* person's point of view and will be flexible enough to resolve matters in an amiable way *both* will gain in the end

Kibbud Av Vo'aim

A wife's main duty is to look after her husband and to run her house efficiently. To achieve this, the Torah freed a married woman from the mitzvo of kibbud av vo'aim during the time she has to devote herself to her husband. This means that if there is a clash between her obligations towards her husband and towards her parents, her husband comes first.(15)

CHAPTER TWO

CONDUCT OF TZNIUS FOR HUSBAND AND WIFE

Introduction

The guidance given in the following chapter is based on the *Shulchon Oruch* and *Chazal* and *seforim kedoshim*. Men have access to these *seforim*, but do not always get round to learning them from the source. There is, therefore, a lot of ignorance in this area regarding what the *Shulchon Oruch* and the Torah attitudes are. This applies even more to some *kallos* and women who do not get a full preparation for a Torah married life.

Many *kallos* enter marriage with a misconception regarding the holiness of the Torah marriage and, when they face realities, come down with a bump. Such *kallos* will find this chapter not only informative, but also supportive, as they will be given the confidence to face, in the right way and spirit, what they will be experiencing.

However, there are some large *heimishe* circles who have other traditions and guidelines; they should continue to follow these.

The uniqueness of the Jewish People lies in their ability to live a normal mundane life, which is nonetheless elevated by the guidelines of the *Torah*. For, the *Torah* encompasses all aspects of married life by teaching what is permitted and what is not (i.e. the law of *nidoh*) and **how** to conduct married life (i.e. the *mitzvo* of *oinoh* and related subjects). Concerning the latter we distinguish between *dinim*, which are compulsory, and attitudes and modes of behaviour which are desirable but *not* compulsory. The purpose of these *dinim* and attitudes is to refine a person and to transform an apparently difficult *mitzvo* into a *mitzvo* replete with meaning and *kedusho*.

Marriage should be utilized for raising one's level of refinement and *kedusho*. Although the *Torah* makes allowances for the weakness of human nature as *Chazal* say: "A man and his wife may do, if he wants, whatever he desires",[1] this permission must be regarded as being directed only to those who have not yet attained a more desirable level.[2] This needs to be so because the *Torah* addresses every kind of person, be he learned or not, the refined and, also, the unrefined. (For full details see pages 118 – 121)

Kedusho

We say in the *b'rochos* under the *chupoh* that *Hashem* created *ahavo* (love), *achvo* (brotherliness), *sholom* (peace) *ve'reus* (and friendship). *Ahavo* (love) between husband and wife is the aim and the ideal status. The other attributes supplement it. Love can manifest itself in a number of ways:- by mutual companionship and *by the way* they interact e.g. *how* one speaks to and feels for the other. There are also other manifestations of love. Just as a loving mother has an urge to kiss her child, so too love in marriage needs to be expressed in a physical manner, at appropriate times.[3]

Due to the inherent *Tznius* of Jewish daughters and the *kedusho* of newly married *bnei Torah* there will be some shyness about this side of marriage. This is to be expected. Time must be allowed for this relationship to develop naturally.

Hashem made it so that as the marriage grows, the wife develops a feeling that she needs the moral support of her husband and his physical closeness. A husband who understands this will give his wife due attention. Failure to do so may result in an emotional explosion on her part, sooner or later.

In spite of this, men must beware to act only within the limits of their *kedusho* and *taharoh*. They must remember that the *tachlis* (purpose) of a wife is to be an *ezer* (help) to her husband so that he will reach a greater level of *kedusho* than he possessed hitherto.[4] Some men are prone to be more excitable than others and physical closeness may even bring them to sin (except at the appropriate times). There is a danger, also, that what started as *chesed* may develop into self-centered indulgence, for, the dividing line between *chesed* and self-indulgence is very fine.

Tznius

Tznius has its application for both even within marriage, and even in respect of the *mitzvo* of *oinoh*.[5] *Tznius* is needed for giving the physical union a spiritual meaning, i.e. to enhance their inner unity. This manifests itself as doing *Hashem*'s wish — albeit with an inner sense of slight hesitation, so as not to be driven by one's instincts. This feeling must not be applied in the wrong way. It should be inside them but should **not** be displayed vis-a-vis his or her partner. For, the danger is, that it could be interpreted by the other as meaning: "You do not care for *me*".

Dinim of *Tznius*

1. During the time of the actual *oinoh* (intimacy) the room must be dark. It does not matter if light shines into the room from outside, as long as it does not shine onto them.[6]

2. *Oinoh* is not permitted during day-time. (A rare exception would be **if this would be the ONLY way to save the husband from sin, but not otherwise.**) Even then, the curtains would have to be drawn and they would also have to cover themselves with a blanket or sheet up to and over their heads, for reasons of *Tznius*.)[7]

3. A *sefer*, *siddur* or *tefillin* must not lie in the room, unless there is a double cover over it e.g. two sheets of paper or a folded towel. If there are open *seforim* shelves in the room, e.g. when they are not in their own house, two curtains or sheets must be hung up in front of them.[8]

4. Even during the night *oinoh* may take place only indoors and never, חס ושלום, in the open (e.g. an isolated place).[9]

5. They need to wash their hands after the termination of the *oinoh*, before they go to sleep (*krias shemah al hamittoh* is to be said beforehand but *hamapil* afterwards[a]).[10]

6. They must not converse during the time of *oinoh* and not talk about general matters shortly before, so that they do not come to think about other people.[11]

7. If his wife is not in the right frame of mind (and

---

a) **Some wash their hands also beforehand. The first *parshoh* of *shemah* should be said again before going to sleep.**

certainly if she is not responsive at all) it would be up to the husband to coax her into **full** agreement.[12] (See also "Motivation and Attitudes" §7)

8. It is a great *avairoh* for either of them to refuse the other, either with the intention of tormenting him or her or for selfish reasons, e.g. when one is tired.[13]

9. *Oinoh* must not take place if other people can overhear them. If children share the parent's bedroom, the parents would have to wait until the children are asleep. One should be careful regarding this even with a baby, if possible.[14]

Motivation and Attitude

1. Their motivating thought should be, ideally, to fulfill the will of G-d who willed their union. By doing the *rotzon Hashem* in the right way they add to the stabilizing of their marriage.[15]

2. They should be motivated, also, by their desire to fulfill their marriage obligation[16] i.e. the *mitzvo* of *oinoh*. This obligation is mandatory *on both* of them even when a woman is pregnant and when she has reached the menopause[17] (except for medical reasons).

3. This motivation should be accompanied by a desire to act with *chesed* towards the *other*, in addition to satisfying one's own desires. The more *chesed* one invests in the other the greater the *mitzvo*. To show little emotion reduces the value of the *mitzvo* and one would fail in achieving its full purpose.[18]

4. The *chesed* aspect must never be underestimated or neglected. It is extremely vital, for this reason, that the timing of *oinoh* should be when each one is alert enough to respond physically and emotionally to the other, not

late at night.

The *Torah* expression of עונתה - "her time" and the prohibition of לא תגרע - "not to reduce", could be applied also to the factor of correct timing. One would have to balance *other* personal or even spiritual considerations against this. Men who are in doubt about the right balance should discuss it with a *Rov*.[19]

5. Their motive should be also, when appropriate, to fulfill the *mitzvo* of bringing children into the world.[20] The quality of one's children with regard to good *midos* and the holiness of their *neshomoh* is dependent on their right thoughts and on the *Tznius* of husband and wife *at that time*. Their foremost thought and longing should be to have the *zechus* to beget children who will have *yir'as shomayim* and who will be *talmiday chachomim*. By picturing great *tzadikim* and by having an inner desire that their children should follow in their footsteps they will influence the kind of child they are going to have.[21]

6. It is customary for them to be covered with a sheet or blanket (up to their neck, at least) even if the room is dark.

7. According to the *Torah* approach the husband is meant to take the initiative and to win first his wife's maximum affection. Possible misunderstandings should be cleared up so that nothing which could interfere in reaching a full inner closeness will stand between them.[22]

8. Every precaution must be taken so that their thoughts should be *only* on their partner, and on no one else. For this reason they should refrain from talking about other people just beforehand, but only about **personal** matters.[23]

9. It is the beauty of a Jewish wife to be shy and reserved,

a stance which is to be maintained even in the inner quarters of her home. Nevertheless, she has to play her part in setting her husband in the right mood. Men are responsive to the nice appearance of their wife. She should make an effort, therefore, to be well dressed and to make herself attractive, even if she is tired.[24]

Generally speaking, a woman should *always* be well dressed when her husband is at home.[25] This will make *her* feel good and will help to promote good relations. She should keep it up even if she **never** hears a compliment because husbands *always* notice it, but may be shy to compliment.

10. The *mitzvo* of *oinoh* was designed, also, to promote a strong bond between husband and wife. Their closeness would be maximized by complete body touch, which would be achieved by the absence of any clothes, to be taken off, though, under a cover or a sheet.[26] This suggestion may not yet be acceptable by some at the beginning of the marriage; it need not be emphasized then, as it is not a major matter.

11. A husband should be sensitive to the feelings and emotions of his wife at all times, but especially at the time of *oinoh*. Her emotions take time to abate and he should show sensitivity to this.[27]

12. Men must be careful not to over-indulge even at the appropriate times, because this would reduce their strength.[28] It may cause them to be ineffective or over-tired the following day with the result that they would not be able to do justice to their obligations towards their employer or *kolel*. The wife, also, needs to be aware of this so that she should not ask for more than he can give.[29]

The Designated Times for *oinoh*[b]

1. The amount of nights which a husband has to set aside
    for his wife's *oinoh* depends on the husband's
    circumstances i.e. whether he works out of town or in
    town.[30]

2. The generally accepted time for a *ben Torah* is twice a
    week, once during the week and once on *Shabbos*.[31]
    This is also the norm for other people who work in
    town.[c]

3. The *t'viloh* night and the night before a person leaves
    for a journey are also compulsory, and are in addition to
    the normal times.[32]

4. When a husband notices that his wife is longing for him,
    he **must** satisfy her.[33] This applies especially when he
    returns from a journey.

5. The times of *oinoh* should be kept up even during the
    time when a wife is pregnant, unless when she feels very
    uncomfortable.[34]

6. *Oinoh* is not permitted on *Yom Kippur*, *Tish'oh B'Av*
    and during the time when either the wife or the husband
    is keeping *shiv'oh* (i.e. the seven days of mourning).[35]

7. A *kallo* may not exactly know what *oinoh* means, but
    she should accept that this is the way *Hashem* planned
    the complete union of husband and wife, though we do

---

b) Intimacy.
c) One should try to keep to this minimum, but it would not be against
halocho to increase it, if either the husband finds it difficult to control
himself or if the wife needs more attention than other women. He should
be careful, though, not to make this a habit as he could become a slave
to his desires. *Chazal* said that **self-control** leads to a decrease of his
desires (מרעיבו שבע).

not understand **why**. She should also know that this is the only way in which a woman can become pregnant.

CHAPTER THREE

THE TORAH VIEW
ON FAMILY
PLANNING

Family planning, as understood normally, has no place in the Jewish marriage. There is, in fact, a rabbinical command for every man to establish a large family, if he and his wife are able to do so.[1] The Rambam and the *Shulchon Oruch* write that a man ought to get married at the age of eighteen because of the principle of זריזים מקדימים למצוה which means that one should not delay the *mitzvo* of פרו ורבו (to be fruitful and multiply) unnecessarily.[2]

Study of Torah and learning a profession are acceptable reasons for delaying marriage, unless one would be able to receive parental or other support.[3]

Contraception

The use of contraception[a] is not permitted, in ordinary

---

a) Besides the consideration of preventing pregnancy, the forms of

➤

circumstances, even if only the Pill.[4] If a wife needs a rest from childbearing for medical reasons, both a doctor (who appreciates the Torah viewpoint) and a Rabbi must be consulted to establish whether, in fact, an exception could be made and what form of contraception would be most appropriate from the *halocho* point of view.[5]

Note: Even in cases where contraception is permitted the law of *nidoh* does still apply.

Sterilization

Sterilization of the female, as an option for preventing pregnancy, could be considered in exceptional circumstances, especially if temporary sterilization is under consideration. A Rabbi should be consulted if the need arises.[6]

Sterilization of the male is categorically[b] forbidden, even after he had a number of children. (A Jewish surgeon must not perform sterilization even on a gentile.)

Abortion

Abortion is normally not permitted, except if the life of the expecting mother is threatened.[7]

In a case where the doctors have advised that the pregnancy will definitely result in the birth of a deformed or subnormal child or in the case of an illegitimate child, a Rabbinical authority, qualified to decide on such questions, must be consulted.

It is understandable that a deformed or subnormal child can be a very great burden to parents, but many parents **have** faced the realities of such a situation and have brought up their child lovingly. Nowadays, one may get help, advice and

---

contraception used by the male border on the prohibition of wasting semen.[4] If a doctor recommends the testing of sperm a Rabbi should be consulted how this problem should be approached.
b) unless his life is endangered.

support from organizations who specialize on such children and, in extreme cases, one could find parents who foster such a child.

LIFE IS TOO PRECIOUS TO DENY IT TO EVEN SUCH A CHILD.

CHAPTER FOUR

THE CONCEPT
OF TZNIUS

What is *Tznius*?

Tznius is an all-embracing concept which is one of the most beautiful *midos* of women. The term *tznius* comes from the Hebrew root צנוע which means "hidden" or "sheltered". The whole point of *tznius* is that a girl or a woman should behave in such a way as to suggest that she shuns publicity and prefers not to be noticed.[a] When she walks on the street her resolve should be "I do not want to attract attention."[b] This is the true basis of *tznius* and all else flows naturally from this concept. A truly modest woman feels no sense of denial or frustration at having to follow the dictates of the Torah in

a) For she is like a princess – and all the princess's glory is within. This is a woman's strong point, as we read in *Yalkut Vayero* on the *possuk*: "Where is Sarah, your wife?" "She is in the tent".
b) On the subject of Dino, the daughter of Yaakov, our Rabbis asked, "What caused her to fall into the snare of Shechem? Because *she went out* – as the *possuk* says: ותצא דינה".

this sphere.[c] Nor will she allow a misplaced expression of *tznius* to prevent her from sometimes acting in ways which are obviously removed from *tznius*, in accordance with the needs of the moment![d]

Tznius in Practical Manifestations

Tznius is demonstrated in the following ways:

(1) *The way one walks* – This should be quiet and unobtrusive, without any attraction-seeking mannerisms (perhaps looking a little downwards, in the manner of modest women), especially if men are passing her.

(2) *Clothing* – Clothes should be of modest cut and refined colours. (See Chapter 5, page 131)

(3) *Speech* – One should adopt a quiet tone, with a refined choice of expressions. (Her voice should not be heard at the back of the room or on the other side of the street.)

(4) *Conduct* – This should be modest but at the same time pleasant and friendly.

---

c) *Rabbenu Yona* writes in his *Igeres Teshuvo*: A woman must be modest, and take care that men other than her husband do not look at her, for she may cause them to sin.

Even between husband and wife there is a place for modesty, as Rashi explains in *Bereshis* 12:11, that Avrohom had never truly recognized Soroh's great beauty due to the modesty that existed between them.

d) It is written in *Yalkut, Bamidbar* 27: "In that generation the women repaired what the men breached". Ahron said: "Take off your golden nose rings" (to make the golden calf) but the women did not wish to do so, and they opposed their husbands. The men did not want to enter the Holy Land but the women (the daughters of Tzlofchod) asked for their portion of Eretz Yisroel.

We learn in *Yalkut, Shoftim* 84, that the husband of Devoro was an ignoramus. She said to him, "Come, I will make wicks and you go and bring them to the *Bais Hamikdosh*." She made the wicks especially thick so that they would give out a lot of light. G-d, who knows the thoughts of people, said to her, "You had the intention of increasing My light—I will surely cause your light to shine in Judah and Israel."

These categories cover all aspects of the standards of general behaviour for girls and married women alike.

Tznius is highly becoming to a woman, and indeed enhances her innate femininity. We say this, despite modern tendencies to downgrade the natural sense of *tznius* in women, and the subsequent sweeping away of all barriers of reserve and shame in society at large.

A married woman imbued with *tznius* dresses nicely with one thought paramount in her mind — to please her husband and she does not allow her standards of modesty to fall when she is outside her own house. Even going into the street should be viewed by her as an unavoidable infringement on the aristocratic status of the Jewish woman (כל כבודה בת מלך פנימה), especially nowadays, as society has relinquished all standards of decency.

Any girl or woman who works outside the home must pay particular attention to *tznius*. Her desire to make a good impression at work should never lead her to compromise on the Torah-given standards of *tznius*.

Tznius — Not a Jewish Invention

Tznius, as such, is not a concept which is confined to the Jewish nation. In fact, when we look at photographs or pictures of bygone eras we are immediately impressed by the general level of modesty. Sadly, this is no longer so, nowadays, and the deterioration in moral standards can be traced directly to a general loss of faith in G-d. Believing that man is descended from the ape is certainly not conducive to maintaining high standards of moral conduct. Unfortunately, these general trends have had their pervasive effect on Jews too, and even on the Orthodox section.

One can say with certainty that *tznius* is one of the main methods through which an individual woman acquires refinement and a measure of self-dignity.

Our position on these matters should however be dia-
metrically opposed to the general consensus of opinion,
knowing as we do that there is a Creator, and possessing the
Torah which governs our daily behavior.

The Torah also informs us that Chavo was created for a
particular task, as is explained in the *Yalkut*:

> *G-d did not create the woman from the head of
> Odom, so that she would not be light-headed; nor
> from the eye, so that she would not be inquisitive;
> nor from the ear, so that she would not be an
> eavesdropper; nor from the hand, so that she would
> not be acquisitive; nor from the foot, so that she
> would not be one who seeks publicity. Rather, she
> was formed from a hidden part of man's body, from
> a rib. Whilst creating each limb, He said to her
> "Be a modest woman!"*

This *Yalkut* demonstrates that *tznius* is a woman's most
central characteristic!

Tznius in the Home

Tznius as a natural sense of shame, should not be
confined to the public arena, but should be adhered to even in
private. For example, even when alone in the house a woman
should not reveal parts of her body which are normally
concealed, if there is no pressing need to do so, even if no one
is around. This should accrue not only from her natural
modesty, but also from her awareness that the Almighty sees
us and knows all our deeds, at all times.[e]

---

e) The *Gemoro* tells us about Kimchis, who said that she merited to
have seven sons, High Priests, because she never uncovered her hair,
even in the privacy of her own four walls. (This is related too about the
mother of the Chazon Ish.)

CHAPTER FIVE

TZNIUS IN HALOCHO

The underlying purpose of the general laws of *tznius* is twofold:

(1) To raise the level of social behaviour and general conduct of man and woman alike.

(2) To delineate certain limits in the sphere of the appearance of women.

In this book we are dealing with the *tznius* of the woman.

Dress

A woman should take care not to reveal even the slightest parts of her body and legs.[a(1)] She should ensure that her dress or

---

a) There are two prohibitions here, both of which originate from the Torah: (1) Because of immodesty; (2) For the sake of 'not putting a stumbling-block before men'.

Any part of the body which is normally covered is considered *ervo*. This must not be judged by present day standards, but rather by the

➤

garment rises up to the neck, both from the front and back. It is permissible to bare the neck itself. The sleeves should cover the elbows at the least.[b] The length of the skirt or dress should allow for adequate covering of the knees even in the sitting position (and even if one wears tights full-length) and the legs must be covered in *opaque*[2] tights.[3]

There are some materials which are not normally transparent but in the sunlight reveal the contours of the body and legs. In a wide garment such as a smock this problem is more common and one should be aware of it as many people fall into this trap through lack of awareness.

One should not tend towards leniency in the sphere of these *halochos* even in an age or locality where they are contrary to accepted practice. Where the *minhag* of the place is to cover parts of the body which the *halocho* does not specify, the *minhag* should assume the stringency of a *din*.

We should mention here the prohibition:

> *A man's garments should not be worn by a woman, nor a woman's garments by a man, for it is an abomination to G-d.*
>
> (*Devorim* 22, 5)

This prohibition applies even when the fashion is that women's clothing resembles that of men (e.g., the wearing of trousers).[c]

Swimming

It is permissible for a girl or woman to swim in the sea or to sun-bathe, but only on a secluded separate women's

---

standards of *tznius* which Jewish girls and women, of the world at large, were accustomed to have.

b) According to the *Mishna Berura*, Chapter 75, sub-paragraph 2.

c) On the subject of women wearing trousers, see *Minchas Yitzchok*, Part 2, 108, and *Igros Moshe, Yoreh Deoh* 1, Chapter 81.

beach, or in a swimming pool at a time set aside for women only.[d(4)]

It is forbidden for men, teenagers, or even younger boys to go to mixed swimming.[e(5)]

Exercising in Front of Men

It is forbidden for a woman to exercise in front of men if she is not dressed in accordance with the *halocho* and it is against the spirit of *tznius* to do so even if she *is* properly dressed. This applies also to dancing at a *chasuno* in front of men.

Hair Covering

Married women,[(6)] widows, or divorced women,[(7)] *must* cover their hair completely when leaving the house[f] or in front of men, but it is the accepted custom to cover one's hair, also *in the house* even in the circle of one's own family.[(8)] The *minhag* is to wear a wig (*shaitel*). Those who are stricter wear other forms of covering.[g]

The wearing of the fashionable long *shaitels* or ponytail wigs is a breach in *tznius*. She may, possibly, fulfill the law but certainly not the spirit of the law. Girls learn in Seminaries much about *emunas chachomim* and *da'as Torah*, if so why, oh why, do they not take notice of the words of our *gedolim*?

Women should exercise strength of character and demonstrate that they **can** withstand the pressure of the surroundings.

---

d) See 1. It seems that if the pool is specified for the use of women, one need not prohibit this although sometimes male pool attendants are present. (There might be a consideration of *tznius*, but not as a matter of law.) A Jewish attendant *is* prohibited to enter therein.

e) The *issur* of looking at parts of the body which are normally covered applies here.

f) *Even Ho'ezer*, Chapter 21, 2, and Chapter 115, 4. This is a Torah prohibition, as is written in *Kesubos* 72.

g) *Orach Chayim*, Chapter 75, באור הלכה ד"ה ודע.

Those who will have the courage to discard the *untzniusdike* wigs can be assured of an unlimited reward in *Olam Habo*!

Not Completely Dressed

It is forbidden to undress completely – even for a moment – in a room where there are *seforim*, unless the *seforim* are covered.[9]

It is permissible for a woman to say a *brocho* (blessing) even when she is not completely dressed or in front of women who are not completely dressed[h] (e.g. when they are swimming).[10]

Singing

It is forbidden for girls from the age of eleven upwards to sing in front of men and it is forbidden for men to listen to their singing.[i][11] It is against the spirit of *tznius* to do so even below that age (unless the girl is very young). Some authorities are lenient with regard to singing within the family circle: i.e. in front of a father, grandfather, son, or brother. Some authorities are stricter in forbidding singing in front of a brother (it all depends upon one's custom).[12]

A husband is allowed to listen to his wife's singing when she is *pure*, but not when he is praying or studying Torah.[13]

---

h) *Orach Chayim*, Chapter 75, 1.

i) The voice of a woman is counted like an *ervo* for a man as it could bring him to unproper thoughts, and is forbidden even at times other than Torah study or prayer. Young girls from about the age of eleven may have reached the age when they menstruate (*Mishna Berura*, Chapter 75, 17) and it is forbidden for men to hear them singing.

CHAPTER SIX

MARRIED PEOPLE VIS-A-VIS OTHER MEN OR WOMEN

One must not assume that by being married one loses one's natural feelings towards the opposite sex. This is not so.

Therefore, a man or a woman[1] must not kiss, embrace or touch purposely[2] or shake hands[3] even with a relation which he or she would not be permitted to marry. This includes a girl over the age of three and a boy over the age of nine. The exception is a daughter or granddaughter, a mother or a grandmother, but not uncles or aunts, nieces or nephews, a daughter-in-law or a mother-in-law.[4] For full details see Chapter 7.

A girl from the age of approximately eleven upwards is likely to have reached the age of menstruation, and she must be treated in this respect like an *ervo*. This means that, with the exception of her father and grandfather, it would be a great sin for a man or boy to kiss or touch her purposely or shake hands with her.[5] This is forbidden, in any case, even at an earlier age, to prevent a man from coming to bad thoughts.

an earlier age, to prevent a man from coming to bad thoughts.

A married or unmarried man must certainly not kiss etc.
a **married** woman, even if she is not related to him. This
prohibition applies to both the man and the woman.[6]

A Fiancé and his Bride

No leniencies exist before or during the time people are
engaged until after the marriage. The fiancé must treat his
bride, in this respect, as a stranger. This prohibition is in force
even if a mature man is engaged to a mature woman who is
past her menopause, irrespective of whether she is a spinster,
widow or a divorcée.[7]

Medical Attention

A doctor is allowed to examine a woman for medical
reasons[a]. Similarly a man may receive medical treatment from
a female doctor or nurse, or be nursed by her when he is ill. [8]

When a woman visits a male doctor or a man visits a
lady doctor they must beware that there should not be a
circumstance of *yichud*.

---

a) but it would be preferable to register with a lady doctor.

CHAPTER SEVEN

KISSING
RELATIVES

Introduction to the Laws of Kissing Relatives

In these introductory notes we shall give the basis on which these *halochos* are built. In the last chapter we touched briefly on the basic *halochos* of kissing relatives. In this chapter we shall go into details of how the *halocho* applies to the different categories of relations and the different ages of boys and girls in relation to this *halocho*.

Blood Relations and Non-blood Relations

Only blood relations possess a **natural** feeling of relationship with their relatives, but even with them, the *halocho* distinguishes between very close relations, such as parents, and not so close relations, such as uncles or aunts.

Cousins and nieces are considered, in this respect, like non-relations, as according to Torah law, cousins may marry one another and an uncle may marry his niece.

When a father kisses his daughter or a son his mother, there is no fear that he will come to any sinful thoughts. But this does not apply to relations which are not so closely related.

Stages of a Girl's Maturity

According to *halocho* a girl is considered theoretically "fit for marriage" from the age of three upwards. (What *chazal* say needs no proof, but it will help people to understand this better when thinking of the high incidence of men abusing very **young** girls.)

As a girl gets older she becomes more attractive to men. The *halocho* considers the approximate age of six or seven as a further stage of maturity and the age of eleven plus as a time where she has almost reached womanhood.

A Boy's Age of Maturity

A boy reaches the stage of being theoretically "fit for marriage" when he reaches the age of nine.

Kissing Relatives — when allowed and when not

1. **Parents and grandparents** are allowed to kiss their children and grandchildren, even when they grow up and even when they are married.[1] This does not apply to adopted or step-children[2] — a boy may be kissed by his step-mother only up to the age of nine and a girl may be kissed by her step-father only up to the age of eleven, both dates exclusive.[3]

2. **Children and grandchildren** may kiss their parents and grandparents even when they are over *bar/bas mitzvo*. This does not apply to adopted or step-children. A girl, from the age of eleven upwards, may not kiss her step-father and a boy, from the age of nine upwards, may not

kiss his step-mother.[4]

3. **A brother** may kiss his younger sister up to the approximate age of ten.[5] This does not apply to a step- or an adopted sister. He may kiss her only up to the age of five or six.[6]

4. A girl, even over the age of *bas mitzvo*, may kiss her brother up to his *bar mitzvo*.[7] In the case of a step- or adopted brother, she may kiss him only up to the age of nine.[8]

5. **The father's or mother's brother** may kiss his niece up to the approximate age of ten[9], but not after that.[10]

6. **An uncle by marriage** may kiss his niece only up to the approximate age of six, preferably only up to the age of three.[11]

7. A girl who is *bas mitzvo* must not kiss any of her uncles.[12]

8. **The father's or mother's sister** may kiss her nephew only up to the age of *bar mitzvo* and vice-versa (but not after that).[13]

9. **The father's or mother's brother's wife** (an aunt only by marriage) must not kiss her nephew once he has reached the age of nine, and he must be trained not to kiss his aunt by marriage.[14]

10. **A father-in-law** must not kiss his daughter-in-law and vice-versa.[15]

11. **A mother-in-law** must not kiss her son-in-law and vice-versa.[16]

12. **A brother-in-law** may not kiss his sister-in-law after the age of three, and a sister-in-law must not kiss her brother-in-law after he has reached the age of nine.[17]

CHAPTER EIGHT

ADOPTED AND STEP-CHILDREN

Status

The feeling of parents towards their children is instinctive and 'parental' in character. But the love of foster parents or of those who adopt children may well be genuine and sincere but it cannot be parental. Accordingly, the Torah recognizes as parents only those who begot[a] the child.[1]

The implications are manifold. Since adopted or step-children are not [b]blood relations the laws of *yichud*, which normally do not apply to one's own children, must be upheld. For example, an adopted son, over the age of nine, may not live at home together with his mother if the father is out of

---

a) As far as the Jewish law is concerned, adoption has no validity in ensuring that the child will become his heir.

b) They may even marry each other.

town. The same applies to an adopted daughter over the age of three and her father.[c(2)]

Also, once a girl reaches the age of eleven (the time when she may have started to menstruate) and a boy the age of nine, the adoptive father may no longer kiss or embrace his daughter and the mother her son because of the *aroyos* laws (see Chapter 6). This applies even where the child is not aware that he is adopted. These difficulties should be taken into consideration when adoption is planned.

The above applies also to step brothers and step sisters or to those who are brothers and sisters by adoption. In *halocho* they are considered as being unrelated and they must comply with the *yichud* and *aroyos* laws.[(3)]

Note: Prior to adopting, it is advisable to ascertain the child's origin (*yichus*) in order to ensure that it is a *kosher* Jewish child.

---

c) Adopting a brother **and** his sister would be a possible solution for the problem of *yichud*.

GUIDANCE TO
SHOLOM BAYIS

CHAPTER NINE

LOOKING FORWARD TO MARRIAGE

It is a fact borne out by experience that any task which we tackle in life needs adequate preparation — and the better prepared we are, the more likely we are to succeed. Strangely, however we tend to overlook this simple truth in one of the most central areas of our lives — marriage. Are our young people adequately prepared for marriage — we may well ask ourselves? This question assumes more force when we consider that marriage is a totally different state to being single. It is a new way of life — in which one becomes a partner rather than a free agent and in which sharing is the operative word. Put this way, it would seem a most daunting task. How can we do our best to ensure its success? As is to be expected, our Rabbis had something to say on the matter.

They gave us clear guidelines as how best to establish and maintain a peaceful home atmosphere.

(1) The first principle is that a man should respect and honour his wife more than he cares about himself.

(2) The woman on the other hand, should try to carry out her husband's wishes wherever possible.

So with these two sides of the coin — a husband whose uppermost concern is his wife's welfare — and a wife whose constant goal is her husband's well-being — one is ensured the most blessed of states — "marital felicity."

There are three foundations for a Jewish home: generosity of spirit, kindness and peace-seeking ways.

An individual who is not prepared to be lenient at times, can never achieve a successful marriage. Likewise, one who has no real kindness in his heart cannot feel true love. Finally someone who is not peace-loving will become embroiled in petty arguments and a tranquil home-life will not ensue.

It is only the individual, who is prepared to heed the advice of our Rabbis, who will achieve the ultimate goal — a truly happy, Jewish home!

The wife of a *talmid chochom*

The next few paragraphs are addressed to those girls who aspire to marry a *talmid chochom*.

Nowadays, when it is common that young men continue their Torah-studies even after marriage, the bride must be prepared and qualified to assume the rôle of the wife of a *talmid chochom*.

The wife of a *talmid chochom* should be aware that learning-time is not limited to his hours in *yeshiva* or *kollel*. No, on the contrary, he uses every spare moment to learn Torah! It is quite possible therefore, that even at mealtimes, or when travelling he will have a *sefer* in his hand. A woman, who understands that Torah-study is the "best merchandise" will be happy with this state of affairs — and will not dream of disturbing him with trivial matters. On the contrary, she will try to shield him from unnecessary disturbances — **his** Torah-study is her first consideration.

Often, the wife of a *talmid chochom* will need to forego a life of luxury and ease and sometimes she may have to make do with very little.

Every girl who reaches the age of looking for a *shidduch* must make a clear decision about her preference: Does she want a life of material ease, or a life of Torah?

By marrying a *talmid chochom* she will acquire the blessings implied in the verse:

> "*It is a tree of life to those that grasp it (the Torah), and all who support it are happy*" (משלי ג', י"ח) and she will gain the unlimited treasures of the World to Come".

We cannot be in much doubt about the decision of a girl who has learned about the greatness of Torah!

CHAPTER TEN

THE ASPIRATIONS OF YOUNG SINGLES BEFORE MARRIAGE

A girl's aspirations

Prior to her marriage, a girl usually has a secure set-up at home. Her father (or mother) supports and looks after her and he (or she) concerns himself (or herself) with her needs! The daughter-father (mother) relationship is a close one, which does not enter the sphere of intimacy.

She hopes for something else, after her wedding day. An intimate relationship with her husband— in which he will in addition take over some aspects of the daughter-father (mother) relationship! It is to her new husband that she will now look for financial and emotional support. He will lead the household and provide solutions to any problems which may arise. She also hopes that her husband-to-be will display good character-traits in showing her both sensitivity and understanding. Finally, she wishes him to be replete with Torah wisdom.

This is a 'tall order' for any young man but he must try his best not to disappoint her. Insofar as he succeeds in fulfilling these hopes, to this degree, she will learn to trust and respect him and — in turn, to seek the best **for** him.

The young man's hopes

Chazal have a saying:

> *"A man without a wife lives a life devoid of good — devoid of joy, blessing, Torah learning, harmony, companionship, the ability to receive atonement!"*

(ילקוט בראשית ב', כ"ג)

Any single man hopes to attain some of the blessings which are denied to him prior to marriage.

However, the above dictum of *Chazal* seems to imply that it is possible, to obtain any of these benefits through the means of **any** fitting woman, no matter of what exact type. However, it is to be expected that a young man should want to choose the finest bride, endowed with the best possible *midos*, and Torah outlook.

CHAPTER ELEVEN

UNDERSTANDING ONE ANOTHER

It is a well known fact that a person's understanding of his fellow-man is drawn from his own experience of the world. For example, how do we apprehend the notion of hunger. We know ourselves that if we miss a meal we experience unpleasant pangs. This knowledge in turn creates a feeling of sympathy with our fellow human-beings who may find themselves in such a plight. But this 'sympathy' springs directly from our own self-knowledge.

It works this way with other human-emotions too — joy, mourning, contentment and frustration — feelings of faith and lack of faith, hope and despair, love and hate, contentment and jealousy. We understand all these feelings in others — simply because we experience them on our own passage through life.

It is this self-knowledge too, which makes us refrain from wounding another person's pride — or allows us to help others in need.

This concept is all-important too, in the sphere of man-woman relationships. However, here it becomes more complicated. For, we cannot rely entirely on extrapolating our own feelings — since men and women are completely different creatures.

They differ in many respects:- in their character-traits, temper, outlook, feelings and the bent of their thoughts.

However, if we find this fact depressing there is one consolation. *Chazal* have paved the way for us in this area of our lives too and if we follow their teachings, we can be sure to find the right path.

Differences between men and women

By being aware of some basic differences between a man and a woman, as spelt out by *Chazal*, husband and wife will be able to understand and better tolerate one another.

Women	Men
Women tend to apply their emotions even to the exercise of the intellect	Men generally judge occurrences objectively
Emotional evaluation takes precedent over intellect	Intellectual evaluation takes precedent over the emotions

These very basic differences come often to the fore when a husband and wife discuss an issue and cannot agree. The husband is astonished that his wife cannot understand matters which to him seem utterly rational and straightforward, however many times he explains them to her. She for her part, cannot see his point of view — at all — and all his (intellectual) arguments fail to impress her. For, whereas the man will look at matters in a rational sense — the woman will in addition, use her deeply-rooted intuition.

In most cases she cannot describe how this intuitive process works — it is something very deep and essentially inexplicable — and this makes it even more difficult for her husband to understand her.

Women	Men
Women are not easily pacified (*Bereshis Rabbo* 82)	A man is easier to appease than a woman. (*Yalkut Bereshis*)
Result: If a woman becomes angry it is difficult to pacify her. (*Bereshis Rabbo* ibid)	Result: If a man is in a temper, he is easy to pacify. Men tend generally to feel more pity for their children, than their wives. (*Tehillim* 103, 13 See *Yalkut* ibid)
Women possess an extra 'understanding'. (*Shabbos* 95)	
Women's judgment is superficial. (*Shabbos* 33; *Kidushin* 80)	

It would seem at first glance that these last two statements contradict one another. On the one hand, we speak of women as possessing an extra measure of understanding, yet we say that they are superficial. It is possible, however, to resolve these difficulties according to the interpretation of the *Chasam Sofer*. (*Nidoh* 4:5):-

Chazal have stated (*Ovos* 80:3) "If there is no understanding (בינה) there is no knowledge (דעת); and if there is no knowledge there can be no understanding".

Understanding is the quality with which one attempts to gain a deeper insight into matter. This can quite often lead to an erroneous understanding. Therefore, a person needs to exercise another quality — which is דעת i.e. the quality which is based on practical experience and general intelligence, and the ability to weigh up matters and judge as to the possible outcome. If one does not possess this kind of judgment, then all one's seemingly clever schemes can ultimately prove to be foolish and impractical. In this respect *Chazal* have stated: "Any scholar who has no דעת the value of his understanding is considered as little more than a discarded carcass." (*Midrash Rabbo Vayikra* 1:15) Even an animal is superior, for it has its instincts and acts accordingly in a pattern.

A human-being must exercise his power of דעת — the intelligence and foresight to weigh up the outcome of the proposed courses of action. Using this quality, he will arrive upon the best method in which to bring matters from potentiality into actuality. We can now understand the above-stated *ma'amar Chazal*: If there is no בינה there is no דעת etc.

Bearing this in mind, we can also understand the difference between a man's intelligence and the intuitive insight of a woman's — דעת is an understanding of matters as they stand and judgment for the future (from the root ידיעה) whilst בינה denotes a flash of creative insight (from the word בנין meaning building). The proper course is for sound judgment to precede this intuitive creativity, for then it will have a sound base. But when this intuitive process precedes knowledge or acknowledgment of all the relevant details, it will necessarily result in something very imperfect and untenable.

Now we can better understand *Chazal's* maxim that a woman has an extra measure of perception — yet she is lacking in the ability to judge matters entirely rationally. Only when the two are joined together — the rationality of the man with the woman's intuition will a proper understanding result.

Therefore, *Chazal* have advised the husband to consult his wife on all household matter and they have also stated: "*A woman's wisdom builds her house*". (*Mishle* 14:1)

The saying: "A woman's judgment and resolve is weak" — also implies that women need protection — because it is difficult for them to withstand hardship. We find an illustration of this principle in the *gemoro*, which relates the story of Rabbi Shimon bar Yochai who was fleeing from the ruling power. He did not reveal his hiding-place to his wife fearing that she may not be able to withstand pressure and would reveal his hideout to the king's messengers. (*Shabbos* 33)

Women	Men
A woman understands the nature of guests more than a man. (*Berachos* 10)	

A woman has been granted the special ability to understand the true natures of those that frequent her household. In this respect her understanding is superior to that of her husband and he would be well advised to rely on her judgment of people's character.

Women	Men
A woman is less generous to guests.	

We would find it difficult to accept this statement were it not derived from our *Chazal*. In fact, we learn it from the behaviour of Sarah *Imeinu*. When the angels came to Avrohom, he commanded her to bring **fine** flour. Sarah said "Ordinary flour is quite sufficient." From this we deduce that a woman is generally less generous, when it comes to the entertainment of guests.

Perhaps, this quality stems from the observable fact that women generally do not possess their own wealth. They are dependent on what their husbands give them. Therefore, deep-down the woman is always worried that her resources will not stretch to all her household needs.

Women	Men
A woman cries easily.	A man should always be careful not to upset his wife.

A woman cries more easily than a man because her feelings precede her intellectual understanding and what is said to her goes straight to the heart. Once she is upset it is very difficult for her husband's justifications or explanations to make any impression, even if he assures her that he did not mean it the way **she** took it.

Some women are naturally reserved and do not show their feelings even when they feel hurt. They hide them from their husbands, and one day matters may come to a head and she will simply be unable to contain herself any longer. At these moments — a husband would do well to remember the dictum in *Pirkay Ovos:* "Do not appease a person at the moment of his anger" and the saying in *Mishlai:* "A **soft** answer will appease anger". He should try to ascertain the underlying cause of her depression, because her outburst is only a manifestation of the 'last straw breaking the camel's back.'

Women	Men
Women have the tendency to take things easy and not exert themselves. (*Yerushalmi Pesachim* 1:4)	

It is apparent that the *Yerushalmi* is referring here to a woman's propensity not to finish what she has begun; when things get a little difficult she gives up more easily than a man.

It is a well known observation that it is difficult for a woman to get ready for a certain time!

Women	Men
One should rebuke women with mildness.	One is permitted to rebuke men who transgress Torah-laws, with harshness.

The Almighty Himself has taught us to make this distinction between men and women. The text states: "Thus you shall speak to the House of Yaakov." The term 'speak' is a mild, considerate form, "And tell the children of Yisroel." This refers to the men, to whom one may use harsh words.

Women	Men
Women do not customarily go out of the house to look for guests, for it is not in tune with their innate sense of modesty. "A princess's glory is within." We derive this principle from the fact that *Hashem* did not banish the daughters of *Moav*. The *Moavi* men were banished because they did not go out of their way to welcome *bnei yisroel*. However, the women were not punished, because it is not customary for women to leave their homes to welcome guests.	It is customary for men to look for guests outside the house. This is what Shlomo *Hamelech* meant when he said: "Her husband is well-known at the city gates – he sits with the elders of the city. (*Mishle* 31)

From the aforementioned examples, we derive the ruling that a woman should take great care in matters of modesty, even in cases where the important *mitzvo* of charity is involved.

Modesty

Guidelines for modesty are drawn from the *Midrash*. When *Hashem* created *Chavo*, he pondered on which part of

Odom to create her from.

> *"He did not create her from the head — so that she would not be too frivolous.*
>
> *Nor from the eye — that she should not be too curious.*
>
> *Nor from the ear — that she be one who does not listen to all sorts of talk.*
>
> *Nor from the mouth — that she not be a gossip.*
>
> *Nor from the heart — that she not be jealous.*
>
> *Nor from the hand — that she not be servile.*
>
> *Nor from the foot — that she not go from place to place with news —*
>
> *But from a hidden place (the rib). For every limb He created He said: 'Let her be a modest woman.'"*

(Yalkut Bereshis Perek 3)

The *Oruch Hashulchon* comments on this matter in the *Even Hoezer* that a woman should not accustom herself to going out too much, for her natural environment is the home, and it is here that her true inner beauty can shine farther. If she does go out, it should be mainly for her household shopping and for matters relating to *mitzvos*, such as a *seudas mitzvo*, for a *chupo* or for a *shiva* visit.

Women	Men
A woman takes more pleasure in looking at nice objects, than in eating fine foods. (*Yalkut Esther* Chapter 1)	
Women have a natural desire to	

know everything. Ten measures of conversation were granted to the world. Nine measures were given to women. (*Kidushin* 49)	
It is difficult for women to keep a secret.	
Women are jealous.	
They take pleasure in eating.	
There is no woman who is not concerned with her looks and with jewellery. (*Kesubos* 39)	

Women need a greater amount and a wider variety of clothes than men. Indeed, we know that some women change several times a day. This must be a part of their nature rather than a coincidental finding amongst women. Why do they feel such a strong impulse for acquiring clothing? Perhaps it is connected to the fact that woman was created after man and from **his** rib. She realises that he was the first one in creation. The text states: "I will make him a helpmate" (*Bereishis* 2:18) In the depths of her heart, she senses that she is of secondary importance — and she beautifies herself in order to boost her ego and to win her husband's admiration.

Women	**Men**
A woman is disqualified from acting as a witness.	A man is qualified to act as a witness.

We might well pose the question, why it is that in a case where the Torah requires two witnesses, women are disqualified. In what aspect lies her inferiority to a man in this respect?

Perhaps, this distinction lies in the saying of our Sages which we mentioned earlier that, whilst her judgment is superficial, she has been granted an extra measure of intuition (page 152). We explained also that according to the *Chasam Sofer* דעת implies a grasp of practical applications and בינה as creativity.

Therefore, when a woman is asked to judge a matter which is non-personal, the relevant details may not be grasped by her with total clarity. When asked, for example, to relate what she has seen, her imaginative powers may well come into play and she may recall details which never in fact occurred.

CHAPTER TWELVE

WAYS TO ACHIEVE HARMONY IN MARRIAGE

Chazal tell us that the way to achieve love of one's fellow Jew is by judging others favourably. The love of one's friend can spring only from a sincere recognition of his good qualities. Conversely, the absence of this recognition will lead one inevitably to downgrade others.

Closeness between a couple is built on the self-same foundation — the mutual recognition of each one's good points. This will help one to generally disregard one's partner's faults. However, any realisation that one's partner has faults should lead one to ask oneself "And, after all am I, myself, perfect?"

Marital Harmony

True marital harmony, which *Chazal* envisioned when they stated: "If there is peace between a couple, the שכינה

dwells with them", is not a gift, but comes rather as a result of continuous effort and hard work, by both parties.

Each of the partners must contribute to the achievement of the correct atmosphere of harmony and co-operation, within the home.

The Wife's Rôle

Rabbenu Yona writes: "A woman should be careful to maintain a peaceful atmosphere between herself and her husband. She may achieve this by ensuring that she is beloved and desirable to him. She should on the other hand be modest in her conduct, for in this merit, she will be privileged to raise worthy children."

Again, our Rabbis have advised us that one of the bases of a happy home is that the woman should try to achieve certain goals. She should make sure that she is attractively dressed, at all times. When her husband comes home she should greet him with a pleasant expression and generally act as if she is pleased to see him. She should converse with him amiably and try never to downgrade him (even jokingly!). She should carry out her household duties with enthusiasm, in accordance, of course, with how much free time she has, and also how much energy. The house should be clean and the table set when her husband comes home.

The *Shelah* comments: If the wife tries to show the proper respect to her husband **at all times** — and vice versa — they will eventually attain a higher spiritual love.

The wife should try to obey her husband's wishes. Her dealings with her husband should be pleasant, respectful and modest. She is in charge of his food-preparations and even in this area she should try to please him by preparing food that he likes. In general, she should try to negate her will before his.

When her husband is angry, she should try to appease him and when he is troubled, she should console him. She

should try to be on good terms with his family, even if they
are difficult. If he gives her presents, she should appear
pleased, even if the gift is a small one. She should pray daily
for her husband's success and that of her children, in the area
of Torah and *mitzvos* and in worldly matters.

The Husband's Rôle

We have a tradition from our Rabbis that the husband's
task is to do חסד to his wife and to make her as happy and
contented as possible.

Chazal said that basis of respect for others is to be
humble in one's dealings with them. This applies especially
with members of one's own family.

The basic ingredient for happiness in the home is
kindness in all the husband's dealings with his wife, and
such kindness that expects no repayment.

Another basic duty of the husband is to create a
harmonious and calm atmosphere by speaking pleasantly to
his wife at all times.

Conversation as a means to achieving harmony

Chazal have said: "Anyone who donates a coin to a
poor man is blessed with six blessings. And one who pacifies
him verbally, is bestowed with eleven blessings."

This saying illustrates the tremendous importance of
pleasant speech. A correct mode of speech is a means to
establishing understanding and closeness.

What is the key to its attainment?

The first principle to bear in mind is that no two
individuals are alike and that it is, therefore, impossible to lay
down general rules. It is wise to avoid arguments and
confrontations, in which one tries to enforce one's own
opinion and viewpoint. One should also avoid deriding one's
partner, with sarcasm and mockery.

There is yet another useful hint for the attainment of

unity — the use of the word 'we' instead of 'I', wherever possible. Word usage has a subtle effect on one's feelings, so that in using this term, the couple will eventually come to feel 'as one'. If a problem arises in the household, the husband should always respond with the wording: "Now let us see how we can solve this problem."

A NOTE OF CAUTION

Human beings are notably prone to error — even the best among us! Let us learn, therefore, how best to avoid mistakes by heeding the following advice:

(1) Avoid comparisons

Avoid saying to your spouse: "Why can't you be like Mr./Mrs. so and so ..."

(2) Avoid speaking disparagingly about your spouse's relatives!

Avoid the above **at all times**. It only leads to disagreements and resentments.

(3) Avoid acting in a superior way to your spouse

Do not say: "I know far better then you!" or "Why can you not understand a simple matter like this? You are devoid of sense."

(4) Avoid discussing your spouse with others

Avoid such discussions (even within the family-circle), even when you wish to point out his or her praises. For our Rabbis have warned us: "Discussion about a person's good points will inevitably lead to a discussion of his or her faults. For this will open the channels for gossip, and talk of a degrading nature."

Be careful also to avoid listening to others downgrading your spouse, and certainly never, relate to your spouse what was said to you about him or her.

(5) Never say to your spouse: "I do so much for you and what do I get in return?"

CHAPTER THIRTEEN

THE HUSBAND –
THE CAPTAIN OF
THE HOUSEHOLD

In a business partnership, each partner makes a particular contribution. The same is true in marriage. Each partner needs to recognise the nature of the other's input and appreciate it.

The husband's contribution

The husband is like the captain of a ship, who guides his household. He bears the overall responsibility both in material and spiritual matters. He is responsible ultimately also for the upbringing of his children.

The husband is also charged with creating the home's Torah atmosphere. One of the ways in which to promote this atmosphere is the proper use of the 'Shabbos and Yomtov table.' These should be joyful occasions, with *zemiros* singing and *divrei Torah*. The 'Shabbos table' should be the high point of the week, with all members present and in a relaxed mood. **The *chinuch* value of a properly conducted 'Shabbos table' can be estimated as contributing at least thirty percent of the *chinuch* a father can provide for his child.** This valuable tool should be made full use of, also, for the promotion of family closeness and harmony. These occasions should never be allowed to fall to a mere mundane level of a 'weekday' meal.

From the moment, the glass is broken under the *chupah*, the husband is charged with the responsibility of guiding his household. But where does he draw the experience to do this successfully?

The truth is that most young men must learn this art through trial and error. There is no way of acquiring it other than through personal experience. In this context, one should heed the words of the *Sefas Emes* who interpreted the *Mishna* in *Ovos*: "Appoint for yourself a mentor," in the following manner. Be your own mentor, i.e. learn from your experience and take care not to fall into the same errors, time and time again.

Some guidelines for making decisions

(a)   Do not make any decisions in haste, without proper consideration.

(b)   Ponder long and deeply as to which is the best course to take in a given situation. Use your intelligence, for the Almighty gave it to you for this very purpose.

(c)   Reach a final decision only after having weighed up all the pros and cons of a given situation.

(d)   The husband should not blame his wife for causing them to be in a particular situation, and vice-versa, (even if justified). For it is said of the Torah-life: "All its ways are pleasant and all its paths are of peacefulness."

(e)   Sometimes one should make use of the adage: "To wait,

and do nothing is preferable. What the intelligence alone cannot sort out, time will," for sometimes there is no obvious solution to a problem.

(f)   In minor matters, it is preferable that a couple make their own decisions; for **no one learns without making mistakes**. Someone who is afraid to make decision, and constantly consults others, even on very trivial matters, will never learn how to make his own decisions, and never therefore stand on his own two feet.

(g)   If the matter is an important one, one should consult an experienced person.

(h)   After the couple have received advice from an outside source, they should then think carefully as to whether or not the advice is acceptable to them.

If it proves not to be, they should consult another person, who might be able to explain the original words of advice. Should they still be unhappy, they should consult with yet another party. But the end result should be that they make their own decision. If however, they realize, eventually, that they do not understand the advice properly, but decide to rely on the superior experience and knowledge of the one who offered it, this will also constitute a sensible course of action.

Who to seek advice from

A counsellor needs to be an individual possessing both wisdom and experience. He/she must also be discreet. It is preferable if he/she is well-acquainted with the particular couple. One must also beware of counsellors who try to force others to accept their opinions. An open mind is an obvious asset!

We find in *Tenach* that Dovid *Hamelech* sought the advice of others, even though he, himself was one of the great Torah-sages of his generation. Despite these credentials, he always sought advice from Achitofel and others. From this particular example, we may understand that not every *talmid chochom* is blessed with special wisdom concerning the ways of the world.

It is certainly necessary, sometimes, to consult a noted authority, however at other times it will be sufficient to take the advice of friends or family members.

How to ask for advice

Our Sages have said that "a judge can only give decisions based on the facts as they are placed before him." This is equally true of an advisor. The counsellor will offer advice according to the facts in his possession. Therefore, it is extremely important to offer the counsellor a well-balanced picture, comprising all details and angles of the case, and not to rely on him/her possessing "*ruach hakodesh*". Thus, a shy person, will find it difficult to 'spill the beans' and solicit proper advice. It is better for this type of individual to go to one of his acquaintances for advice.

CHAPTER FOURTEEN

A WOMAN OF VALOUR

The woman bears responsibility for the running of her household. This includes many mundane details. She is responsible for shopping, cooking and baking, laundry, cleanliness and preparations for Shabbos and *Yom Tovim*. If the couple have children, then they are primarily the mother's responsibility. A woman's work is never done! This is a popular saying with more than a ring of truth in it. For she is busy day and night, and her work extends over 365 days of the year, without any real holidays.

Even her mealtimes are not sacrosanct, and she is fortunate if she is able to sit at the table for more than five consecutive minutes, without being summoned to one or other duty.

Even when she is not busy directly with the housework, her thoughts are preoccupied with her husband and children. What will her husband/ neighbours/mother-in-law say about such and such? Her mind is never free of such anxieties.

Sometimes, times are hard and there is little money about.
Yom tov is a time when she might feel financial pressures
more acutely.

We might sum up by stating that the married woman
never knows a moment's real peace of mind, for household
worries pursue her from dusk till dawn. (Contrast this to the
situation of the husband who goes out to his place of work or
study, but is free of these responsibilities when he returns
home!)

CHAPTER FIFTEEN

BASIC NECESSITIES

Chazal say that when a housewife is short of money for buying food for her household she immediately cries.

The *gemoro* states in this vein that "One must try and ensure that there is enough money for all household necessities."

How do we define necessities?

Nowadays, there are many items which women have become accustomed to from home and consider indispensable. Since women usually know more about such matters then men, it is not worth arguing about, and challenging her with statements such as: "Is this really necessary?" After all, *Sholom Bayis* is of paramount importance.

Women do generally demand that their husbands bring in the basic income to the house, as if this is their justifiable right. That this is a natural state of affairs can be proven for the *Midrash* which states:

"Why are prophets compared to women?"

In just the same way as women are not embarrassed to demand financial support from their husbands, the prophets are not ashamed to demand the needs of bnei yisroel form their Father in Heaven.

(Yalkut Yisro)

According to this parable, the prophets ask the Almighty to fulfill the needs of His people, precisely because it lies within His power to do so. In this way, women may only ask of their husbands, what they are able to do. **If the husband is pressed for money, she should not make undue demands of him.**

If one is approached by a poor man and one has nothing to give, it is one's duty to appease the one who solicits funds. He will then understand that one **wants** to give but one simply is unable to. This should be the husband's approach to his wife, at times when he is unfortunately unable to provide her with what she asks.

Duties set out in the *kesubo*

The *kesubo* stipulates that the husband should provide his wife with her basic needs — food, clothing and furnishings. He should try to upkeep her in the style to which she has been accustomed at home.

However, a woman who is fully aware at the outset that her husband has limited means of providing for her, such as a *kollel-yungerman*, is an exception to the above rule.

Generally speaking, since *Chazal* have placed the responsibility for the woman's upkeep squarely on her husband's shoulders, he should not burden her unduly with financial pressures. But these are generalisations, and individual cases obviously vary.

CHAPTER SIXTEEN

HER HOME IS HER CASTLE

The *Rema* writes: "A woman should not become accustomed to going out of the house too much, as it is preferable that she remains in her home-environment. (*Even Ho'Ezer* 73;1)

In practice we are very far-removed from this ideal. The influences of the secular world, in which all barriers of modesty and decency have been broken down, have penetrated even our defenses. However, we must try to approach Torah-true principles, in this important area, as much as possible.

Is it advisable for a woman to go out to work?

The main rôle of the married woman is to run the home, to help her husband, and to bring up her children. There are several tasks which a woman is dutybound to carry out herself, even if she has outside help, among them: to serve her husband his meals and to join him for his meals. According to the *halocho*, she is dutybound even to wash his face and hands, (if he requires her to do so). The intention behind all these actions is that she should endear herself to her husband.

As long as she is required to be 'at the helm' of the household, she should carry out these duties in a pleasant and unbegrudging manner.

But the woman who works a full day outside of the home, is apt to forget or neglect her major areas of responsibilities. At work, she is a free-agent and in some cases is in charge of others, so that it may prove difficult for her then to readjust to a situation whereby she is subordinate in the home.

If she is required in the workplace to have dealings with men, and even to giving them orders, she will need to develop a dominant strain, which is in direct contradiction to the quality of modesty. Also, a woman who goes out to work wants to dress attractively and wear jewellery. If she does so, she ends up dressing in order to create an impression on others rather than for her husband alone.

There is also another side to this coin. By dressing attractively, she is inadvertently arousing the impulses of the men at work. This can misfire and hit the woman like a boomerang. This **has** happened, unfortunately, in the past, even in the case of married women and even in religious circles.

I have been asked to write about this last point, not only for the sake of the women, but also for the sake of the husbands. Men must become more aware that by allowing their wives to work alongside men (or to study alongside men in colleges or universities), they are exposing their wives to the lust of those whose actions are unpredictable. Husbands should consider, therefore, whether taking a job in unsuitable surroundings should take priority over the maintaining their wife's level of *tznius*. Going to work should be confined to places where one knows that those who work there are of reputable standards.

The reality is that nowadays, many women have to go out to work, for a variety of reasons. They must however be extremely careful of the above points, and also bear in mind that the primary task of a wife is to assist her husband **in the home** and to bring up her children **herself**, rather than by a childminder.

CHAPTER SEVENTEEN

THE WOMAN'S SHARE IN AVODAS HASHEM

We accept that there are differences in the service of Hashem of *kohanim* and *yisroelim*. In just the same way, there are distinctions between the woman's service of G-d and the man's.

The main differentiation is that a woman is freed of the obligation of *limud Torah* and from positive time-bound *mitzvos*.

Counterbalancing this, the Torah has placed on the woman the responsibility of seeing to the household needs and the upbringing of the children, a task with which the woman is preoccupied from morning till night. Under these circumstances, it is impossible for a woman to be immersed in spiritual matters, the best part of the day, and this is not her lot.

But how can a woman raise her standard in *yiddishkeit?*

The answer to this is quite simple, her standard is bound

up to that of her husband. If he is enthusiastic in his performance of *mitzvos*, if he is kind and considerate to her and gives her due respect, if he acts with the proper *midos* towards his wife and children and towards his parents, speaking to them amiably and with refinement, she will automatically rise to his level.

But if he tries directly to change her, she may resent it. He will then lose far more than he can hope to gain.

Any intelligent person will weigh up what he may suitably ask of his wife. Nor should he think: "What will I lose by asking her?" For any request which is out of place will cause anger and resentment on her side.

It is a well-known fact that it is difficult for any individual to change the habits of a lifetime. Why expect this of one's wife?

It is true that in the sphere of *minhagim*, our authorities rule that the woman should adopt those of her husband. However, in a case where the wife would be happier if she continues her customs, and therefore *sholom bayis* would be affected, it becomes less clear-cut. (Generally, husbands do not **insist** that their wives adopt his customs, unless they show a ready inclination to do so.)

CHAPTER EIGHTEEN

GIVE AND TAKE

The text states: "It is not good for a man to be alone, I will make him a helpmate."

The *Midrash* comments on these words, that any man who has no wife is:

— *devoid of 'good', as it is written:* "It is not good"

— *devoid of joy, as it says:* "You should rejoice in your household"

— *without blessing, as it says:* "She brings blessing to your house"

— *without Torah, without defenses, without peace, as it states:* "You should know peace in your tents".

In summary, a man without a wife is not a complete person.

It follows therefore, that a woman is responsible for her husband's peace of mind, for without her, he is incomplete.

The *Midrash* states that the man is dutybound to give his wife the proper respect in recognising that she truly completes him spiritually. This is quite apart from the other help that she gives him in household matters, such as cleanliness, washing and cooking and bringing up the children.

It is the duty of every Jew to bring joy to those less fortunate than himself in society, such as widows and orphans or others in need. We well know that it is not the act of kindness itself which is important, but the **way** in which we carry it out. Do we give charity with a smile or in a begrudging, resentful manner? Do we offer a few words of encouragement to the poor, or do we give our donations in sullen silence?

All these principles apply equally to one's dealings with one's wife.

There are *halochos* as to who takes precedence in matters of charity: the poor of your own town come before those in other places; a relation that lives in another town takes precedence over a town-dweller. The rule is that the closer the relationship, the greater, the more pressing your duty. In the case of one's wife whom our Rabbis have described as one's own self, it is obvious that she should be the **first in line** for any of her husband's charitable duties.

Kindness

It is written: "אשרי משכיל אל דל" — Happy is he who acts with consideration towards the poor. (*Tehilim* 41:2) The word משכיל teaches us that one who gives charity must consider what is in the best interest of the poor man.

This is true of any act of kindness. It must be carried out in such a way as to be acceptable to the recipient. The rule is that goodwill alone is not enough — the act must be both helpful and acceptable to the individual at the receiving end. For example, if someone gives a donation to a poor man, who originally came from a wealthy background, publicly and thereby embarrasses him, he loses his reward for the charity. Or, if a hungry person comes asking for bread and one gives him a garment, then even if his intentions are worthy, his actions are not, for his urgent need is for bread.

In the husband and wife relationship, the husband must consider what will please his wife most. If he gives her, for example, an unwanted gift, he has not achieved the aim of affording her true pleasure.

Reb Yisroel Salanter once gave the following response to one of his students who asked him why he had seemingly failed to achieve *sholom bayis*, although in his estimation, he had always treated his wife well: "Kindness is not always what you may term as being good for her, but what she **herself** wishes. You must learn to make this vital distinction," was the wise Reb Yisroel's reply.

CHAPTER NINETEEN

WHO TAKES PRIORITY – HER HUSBAND OR HER CHILDREN

Many women are troubled, even tormented, at times, by the problem of who should come first when she is unable to attend to the needs of all her family simultaneously.

Let us imagine the following:

Her husband comes home in the evening for his supper but his wife is still helping her daughter with her homework. Her instinct draws her towards her daughter. 'Can't he attend to his supper himself?', she thinks. She suggests to her husband to go to the deep-freeze and take out some pre-cooked food and put it into the microwave. He prepares his own supper and eats alone, without her company.

The husband was not happy with this arrangement, but he tolerates this set-up, rather than creating tension in the house.

Was her action correct and appropriate?

Let us analyze this case. All women know that the Torah frees them from looking after their parents, once they get married, at such times when this would clash with the needs of her husband, because it is the primary role of a woman to be an *ezer* to her husband. The status of *ezer* (עזר) must not be interpreted as taking on the position of a maidservant (שפחה). The term עזר has a much higher and more dignified meaning. The word עזר is connected with the word "עוז" – strength. This means that the wife acts as a strength to her husband by always being at his side as a loyal companion and friend. According to the *Midrash* (ילקוט בראשית כ"ג) a man without a wife is lacking in many things:

(a) He cannot be termed as being good.

(b) He has no joy,

(c) he has no blessing,

(d) his Torah is incomplete,

(e) he is without protection from sin and

(f) he is without peace.

The role of a wife, therefore, is to make up for and to complement all those shortcomings by acting as a true companion **whenever** her togetherness would be appreciated. This interpretation is not only based on the *Midrash*, but is a *halocho* in the *Shulchon Oruch*. The *Shulchon Oruch* defines the practical duties of a wife in the following way:

"It is the duty of a wife to assist her husband, to arrange his bed and to prepare his drinks, to serve him during meals and to do small odd jobs for him."

The *Chelkas Mechokek* adds:

"She needs to be ready always to serve him and to join him for his meals." (Even Hoezer *80,4 and* Chelkas Mechokek *11)*

We now have a clear *psak halocho* that a wife has to join her husband for his meals and serve them to him.

If her obligation towards her husband overrides her duty towards her parents, **all the more so does the obligation override the needs of her children.**

In any case, what greater *chinuch* in *kibbud av* can there be for her children than by showing them that their father comes first. By seeing that their mother honours him, they will also honour him. In turn, a husband who has such a supportive wife will surely reciprocate and honour his wife. Again, this will be an example to the children and the whole family will benefit by the role model she sets for them.

CONCLUSION

In conclusion, let us return to one of the sayings with which we began, namely, that the Jewish home is dependent on three essential pillars: generosity, kindness and peace-loving ways. But **both** partners have to be willing to adopt this generous spirit towards one another; both partners' uppermost concern must be the welfare of his or her spouse; both partners have to be kind to one another and both have to positively pursue *sholom bayis*.

With these guidelines fixed firmly in the mind, we are sure that it is within the reach of every Jewish couple to attain and maintain the most pivotal of blessings — true *sholom bayis*!

PART II

מקורות והערות

Hebrew Footnotes

To be read from right to left side of book

להקל עד גיל י"ג בבן אבל לא למעלה מגיל י"ג דלא גרע מאח ואחות דאסור.

14. דאלו אין להן קרבת בשר ואדרבא הן ערוה עליו ולכן אסור למעלה מגיל ט'. ויש לחנכו שלא לנשק אותן כיון דהגיע לחינוך.

15. זה פשוט לאיסור דהרי היא ערוה מדאורייתא (חוץ ממה שהיא ג"כ אשת איש אם לא שמת בעלה). וזה איסור תורה לדעת הרמב"ם.

16. עיין ציון 15) וגם היא ערוה עליו מן התורה.

17. עיין ציון 15) וגם היא ערוה עליו מן התורה.

CHAPTER 8

ילדים מאומצים

ADOPTED AND STEP CHILDREN

1. דלא מצינו לא בגמרא ולא ברמב"ם ולא בש"ע שום מקור שילד יחשב כבנו ע"י הסכמת ב"ד או חוק המדינה. ואף לו יסכימו כל בני המדינה לכך א"א לחדש חוק כזה מדכתיב בתורתנו לא תוסיפו ולא תגרעו ממנו רק מבחינת רוחניות מצינו שכל המלמד את בן חברו תורה כאלו יולדו (סנהדרין י"ט). וכן יש על המאמץ חיובים מוסריים הנובעים מרגש של הכרת הטוב לכבד הוריו שגדלוהו. וגם למגדלים יחשב לזכות "כאילו" קיימו פריה ורביה כדאיתא בסנהדרין דף י"ט ע"ב שכל המגדל יתום בתוך ביתו מעלה עליו הכתוב כאילו יולדו. וע' בחכמת שלמה על אבה"ע סי' א' שחקר אם מקיים מצות פו"ר כשמגדל יתום.

ולעניין ירושה כיון שאינו בנו אינו יורשו. אבל יש אופנים איך להבטיח מחיים שבנו המאומץ יקבל חלק מן הירושה, ויעשה שאלת חכם.

2. כן הסכימו גאוני זמננו. ע' באוצר הפוסקים סוף חלק ט' בדף ק"ל וקל"ב.

3. כג"ל מספר 2.

3. עיין ציון 1).

4. עיין ציון 2). ומה שהבן אסור לנשק את אמו אחר גיל 9 היינו משום שהיא ערוה עליו דהרי היא אשת איש.

5. עיי"ש בחלקת מחוקק סי"ק יי"א דמיסתפק באח גדול אם מותר לשכב במטה אחת עם אחותו הקטנה עד גיל שדים נכונו דהיינו בערך גיל אחת עשרה אבל בנישוק שקל יותר פשוט להיתר כיון דהוה רק בגדר נישוק משפחתי דאף כשששניהם גדולים אינו אלא בגדר "מגונה ביותר ודבר איסור" אבל בקטנה עד אותו גיל מותר.

6. דאחותה המאומצת או אחותה החורגה הרי היא כזרה אצלה ודינה כשאר פנויה דיש להקל עד גיל ה' או ו' הכל לפי גדלה. ולא החמרתי מגיל ג' ולמעלה כיון דאינה ערוה וסוכ"ס מכוון לשם נשיקה משפחתית (אם האמת כן).

7. דבר זה דומה למה שכתבתי בציון 5) דכמו דאח מותר לנשק אחותו הקטנה ה"ה דאחותו הגדולה מותרת לנשק אחיה הקטן עד גיל יי"ג. וזה נלמד ממה שהאם מותרת לשכוב עם בנה אפילו בקירוב בשר עד גיל יי"ג. ולכן אין להקל לגבי אח ואחות למעלה מגיל זה.

8. עיין ציון 6). וכאן מותרת לנשקי עד גיל ט' דהרי זה נחשב כקטן ממש כיון דאינו ראוי לביאה.

9. הנה אח האב או את האם הרי הוא מותר בבת אחותו וא"כ אינה ערוה עליו ונחשבת כפנויה בעלמא. ואף דאין לנשק שאר פנויה בעלמא מחמת היררהור, אבל כאן הנידון בנישוק משפחתי. ואף דלא מצינו קולא מיוחדת בשאר קרובים רק מאח ואחותו, מי"מ יש להקל כיון דאינה ערוה עליהם.

10. אחר גיל יו"ד הרי היא לפעמים כבר בגיל שדים נכונו. וגם יש לחוש שהיא כבר נדה וא"כ נעשית עליו ערוה ולא עדיף מאח ואחות וק"ל.

11. דבעל אחות אביו או בעל אחות אשתו אינם בגדר קרובים אשר אין לבם נוקפו עליהם (עיין במחבר כ"א סעי' ז'). ולכן הרי היא ככל שאר פנויה אשר נזהרים מלנשק אותה מחמת חשש היררהור. ואינו דומה לאח האב או האם דיש להם קירבת בשר.

12. דמאחר שהיא גדולה הרי היא בודאי נדה וא"כ הרי היא ערוה. וא"כ הרי היא בכלל מה שכי' המחבר בסעי' ז' דאף באין לבו נוקפה עליהן הרי זה מגונה ויש איסור עיי"ש.

13. דמאחר דיש להן קרבת בשר והן מתכוונות לנשיקה משפחתית יש

מותרת לשמש את האיש אפילו לשיטת הב"יי והמחבר ביו"יד סיי קצ"יה
סעיי יי"ז האוסר לרופא לשמש הדפק של אשתו אפילו במקום סכנה
כדמשמע שם מן הגריי"א סיי"ק כ', והטעם צי"ל ליצר הרע של אשה
קלוש משל איש וסתם נגיעה לא נחשב מעשה קירוב. וע"י בסי' שלי"ה
בטי"ז שמביא סברה זו.

חזינן מזה דנגיעה שאינה מעשה חיבה בעצם אינה אסורה ובתנאי
שאין לחוש שיתגבר עליו יצרו.

ואם נפלה אשה לארץ וא"יא לה לקום מעצמה מותר לאיש
להקימה וכן כל כיו"יב, מיהו ראוי ליזהר מנגיעת בשר ממש בכל מה
דאפשר.

ג) אין אסור על איש לקבל טיפול רפואית בבית החולים
מרופאה או מאחות בין מישראלית או מנכרית, כיון שאין כאן מעשה
חיבה, וגם אין לחוש שיתגבר עליו יצרו, כיון שהוא במקום רבים ולא
שייך שיבא לידי עבירה, וממילא לא יבא ג"יכ לידי ההרהור עבירה, וכן
כשאשתו עמו מותר לקבל טיפול מן אחות גם בביתו מטעם הנ"יל אף
אם אינו חולה ממש כשא"יא בענין אחר. ויש לדון ק"יו ממה דאיתא
באבהי"יע סיי כ"יא ברמי"יא סעיף ה' די"ש מי שמתיר לאיש לרחוץ במרחץ
שמצויים שם רבים ע"יי שפחה נכרית, ואף שרבים חולקים שם, היינו
משום דסתם רחיצה היא מעשה של חיבה, אבל בחולה או בטיפול
רפואית כי"יע יודו דמותר, והמחמיר עליו גם באופן זה קדוש יאמר לו,
מיהו אם חושש שיתגבר עליו יצרו יחוש לעצמו. ולכן ראוי לבחור בלתי
נשוי להתרחק מזה.

CHAPTER 7
KISSING RELATIVES

1. אהעי"ז סי' כ"יא סעי' ז'. ועי"ש בבי"יש סי"יק יי"ד דאף לאחר
הנישואין מותר. אך כמדומני שהיראים נזהרים בתורת הרחקה
מלנשק את בת בנם או את בת בתם כשהיא מבוגרת וכי"ש כשהיא
נשואה אף שמותר מצד הדין.

2. דמאחר דאין ביניהם קירוב בשר נחשבים כזרים. והחמרתי בבן
שמותרת האם לנשק אותו רק עד גיל ט' דהרי היא אשת איש. אבל
הקלתי בבת עד גיל יו"יד כיון דאינה אלא פנויה האב בודאי אינו
מכוון אלא לשם אהבה משפחתית אין לחוש להרהור.

←

ממנו עכ"ל.

4.   בפ' כ"א מהל' איסורי ביאה הלכה ו' וז"ל: המחבק אחת מן העריות שאין לבו של אדם נוקפו עליהם, אע"פ שאין שם תאוה ולא הנאה כלל הרי זה מגונה ביותר ודבר איסור והוא מעשה טפשים וכו'.

5.   כי נדה בכלל ערוה.

6.   וז"ל רבנו יונה באגרת התשובה דרוש א': ואסור ליגע באשת איש (וה"ה שאר ערוה) בידיה ובפניה או בכל אבר מאבריה מן התורה . . . ומתבאר בסנהדרין דף ע"ה כי ראוי לאדם שיהרג ואל יעבור על זה (אם מכוון להנאה).

ועיין ביורה דעה סי' קנ"ז סעיף א' ברמ"א ובש"ך ס"ק י' ובפ"ת ס"ק יי"א; ועיין חיי אדם כלל כ"ה סעיף יי"ג ובמשנה ברורה סי' שליט בבאור הלכה מה שכתב אודות הריקודים.

7.   כי עדיין היא נדה, והלא אף אשתו נדה אסור ליגע בה; וכ"ש שאסור לנשקה או לחבקה.

8.   א) **ורופא מותר בכל בדיקות שעושים לנשים** ואפילו לנכרית, כמבואר בש"ך סי' קצ"ה ס"ק כ', כי אינו עושה לשם חבה ודרך חיבה, כלומר דעצם הפעולה לצורך רפואה אינה מעשה של חיבה ולכן אינו בכלל לאו דלא תקרבו ואף מדרבנן מותר. והא דלא חיישינן דאולי יבא לידי הרהור (ממילא יהיה אולי ג"כ מעשה של לא תקרבו) היינו משום דעסוק במלאכתו וטרוד במחשבתו. אך צ"ע מה יעשה אם באמת בא לו הרהור.

ב) **ובענין אי יש היתר לאיש לשמש אשה חולה** כשאין שם אחר להקימה וכיו"ב, מבואר בש"ך ובט"ז ביו"ד סי' שליה דמותר, דדוקא כשהיא חולת מעיים יש לחוש יותר להרהור ושיבא לידי עברה, אבל שאר חולה מותר.

ועל דרך זה נפסק בש"ע יו"ד סי' שליה דאשה מותרת לשמש אפילו לאיש חולה מעיים לסייעו להקימו וכיו"ב ואפילו נוגעת בו, והיינו משום דאינה עושה לשם חיבה, גם דאינו מעשה חיבה ואין איסור לא על האשה (אף שגם היא מוזהרת על לאו דלא תקרבו כדלעיל מספר 1), ולא על האיש לקבל שימושה כיון דאינו מכוון ליהנות ממנה, ועייייש בש"ך וט"ז, ומבואר מדבריהם דאיש ג"כ מותר לשמש אשה חולה להקימה ולהשכיבה רק לא בחולת מעיים, כי בחולת מעיים שייך יותר שיתגבר עליו יצרו כיון שמגלית עצמה תדיר, ואשה

⇐

יעבור. והוסיף שאף אם יגרום הלבנת פנים לאשה כשימנע מליתן ידו,
וכגון שהיא מגישה מקודם ג"כ אסור. וכי שחיי לומר שיש צד היתר,
ומביא מגמרא פ"ב דברכות שרב אדא ב"א קרע כרבלתו [בגד חשוב
שאינו צנוע] של אשה בשוק בחושבו שהיא בת ישראל. מיהו כי שיסביר
לאשה בטוטו"ד שהוא אסור גמור כפי הסכמת גדולי הרבנים ולא רק
חומרא. ובנכרית צ"ע אם זה בכלל יהרג ואל יעבור.

א)‏ **ובענין ליתן יד לאחותו.** יש לעיין במה דאינו מבואר בפוסקים
האם יש איזה קולא ליתן יד לאחותו או לאחות אמו או לאחות אביו,
כי קרובים אלו אין לבו נוקפו עליהם; ואף שמבואר ברמב"ם שלא
יקרב עליהם כלל ודבר מכוער לנשק או לחבק אותם, מ"מ כשמכוון
לשם שמים ויש כאן רק נתינת יד מפני השלום ובמקום שיש צורך,
אולי דאין מזניחים למי שרוצה להקל לעצמו.

ב)‏ **אבל פשוט שכל זה אינו שייך בשאר קרובים** כגון אשת אחי
אביו או אשת אחי אמו (דודה), וכי"ש דאין היתר על דוד להקל לעצמו
ליתן יד לבת אחיו או לבת אחותו. וכן אין שום קולא בנוגע לכלתו
(אשת בנו) או לחמותו כי אצל אלו לא נמצא בפוסקים שום קולא, כי
באלו הוא **איסור ממש ולא רק מכוער** כשמנשקים את קרוביהם,
והעולם טועים בזה. וכי"ש שאין שום קולא ליתן ידו לבת דודו, ופשוט.

ג)‏ ובאח ואחות יש אולי מקום להקל, דהא מצינו כמה קולות
אצלם, דהיינו שלא שייך איסור יחוד וכן מותרת לעיין ברישיה
כמבואר בט"ז ובב"ש בסיי כ"א, אלמא דאין כאן איסור התקרבות אף
שעסוקים במעשה חבה, ונתינת יד לא גרע, וצ"ע.

ד)‏ **ואם אח שאינו נזהר בכל זה מקרב עצמו לנשק אחותו,** או
אם אחות אביו או אחות אמו (דוקא אלו ולא שום קרוב אחר)
מקרבת עצמה לנשק אותו, נראה דאין דאין איסור על מי שהוא בשב ואל
תעשה, ואינו מחויב למחות בחוזק יד במקום דרכי שלום, כי רק
מצד המנשק מכוער הדבר.

ה)‏ אבל כשדוד שאינו אחי אביה או אחי אמה רוצה לנשק את
קרובתה מחויבת לסרב. כי שם אסור על פי עיקר הדין.

ובכל האופנים שמותרים על פי דין יש להחמיר ולהתרחק בכל מה
שאפשר (חוץ מאב לבתו והאם לבנה), וכלשון הערוך השלחן בכעין זה,
וז"ל בסיי כ"א סעיף ז': כללו של דבר השם אורחותיו ומעגלותיו לא
יכשל לעולם, ואשר לא ישים אל לבו, יפול ברשת היצה"ר כי חזק הוא

⇐

כתבו דאף אם מותר מן הדין אבל מכוער הדבר. ובשעת תורה ותפילה יש להחמיר יותר; וע' באוצר הפוסקים סי' כ"א סעי' א' ס"ק אות ה'.

12. א) **לגבי אביה וזקינה** פשוט שמותר דהא אפילו חיבוק ונישוק מותר. ומיסתבר דאפילו בשעת תורה מותר דאין כאן דבר ערוה כלל וכמו דמותר האב בתורה אף בשעה שבתו שוכבת אצלו ע"פ התנאים המבוארים באו"ח סי' ע"ג.

13. שם באו"ח סי' ע"ה סעיף ג', וע' במ"ב שם ס"ק י"ז; וכשהיא אינה טהורה ע' ביו"ד סי' קצ"ה בפ"ת ס"ק י' דיש לאסור (דהא גם לגבי בעלה נחשבת קולה כערוה דהא אף באשתו טהורה אין לשמוע קולה בשעה ק"ש ולכן יש מקום לאסור באשתו טמאה כמו כאסור אז להסתכל במקומות המכוסים שלה) ואף שהניח בצ"ע, האחרונים נקטו לאיסור ע' בקצש"ע סי' קנ"ז סעיף י' ועוד אחרונים.

CHAPTER 6
MARRIED PEOPLE VIS-A VIS OTHER MEN AND WOMEN

1. כי לאו דלא תקרבו שייך אף בנשים כמבואר בחינוך מצוה קפ"ח וברש"י בחומש.

2. אבה"ע סי' כ"א סעיף ז' וחכ"א כלל קכ"ה, ולשיטת הרמב"ם פ' כ"א מהל' איסור"ב ה"א עובר בלאו דלא תקרבו ונמשך אחריו הש"ע באבה"ע סי' כ' סעיף א'.

3. **ולענין ליתן יד לאשה** דרך פריסת שלום באופן שאינו מכוון לחיבה לא נמצא בפוסקים מי שמתיר.

א) והטעם, כי נתינת יד לאשה היא בעצם מעשה של קירוב הדעת, ואף דקרוב דאין כאן איסור תורה דלא תקרבו **אם באמת אינו מכוון לחיבה**, מ"מ כתבו הפוסקים דיש איסור דרבנן, ואין דומה לרופא המוזכר בשו"ת סי' קצ"ה ס"ק י'. ועיין בכל זה באריכות בשדה חמד כרך ג' מערכת קי' כלל ז' וכן באוצר הפוסקים סי' כ'.

ב) **ואף אם יעטוף ידיו בבתי ידים** אינו מועיל כמבואר בספר החסידים סי' תתרי"ץ וז"ל: לא יתקע יהודי בכף נכרית ולא הנכרית בכף יהודי אע"פ שהיד מעוטפת בבגד סייג לגילוי עריות ע"כ.

וכעת ראיתי מכתב כתב יד מהרה"ג רי"י קניבסקי זצ"ל (הסטייפלר) שענה לשואל מלונדון שאין שום היתר, והוא חמור כמו חיבוק ונישוק. וכתב בשם גיסו החזון איש זצ"ל שהוא בכלל יהרג ואל

⇐

6. כמבואר באבה"ע סי' כ"א סעיף ב' וסי' קט"ז סעיף ד', וע' חכ"א כלל קכ"ה סעיף ט', והוא איסור תורה כדאי' בכתובות דף ע"ב: "ראשה פרוע דאורייתא דכתיב ופרע את ראש האשה (במדבר ה' י"ח)". והמנהג היום ללבוש פאה נכרית. והפרושים נוהגים בכיסוי שאינו של שער ומקיימים "אל תטוש תורת אמך" ואשרי חלקם.

7. מבואר שם בב"ש ס"ק ה'.

8. ע' בבאור הלכה או"ח סי' ע"ה סעיף ב' ד"ה ודע. ואשה צנועה זוכה לבנים צדיקים.

כדאיתא במס' יומא דף מ"ז, דשבעה בנים כהנים גדולים היו לה לקמחית בזכות שלא ראו קורות ביתה קליעות שערה.

9. הטעם מה שלא תעמוד ערומה נגד ספרים הוא משום בזיון כתבי קודש, ונלמד מדין מזוזה ע' יו"ד סי' רפ"ו סעיף ב' ובט"ז שם סק"ה (ואין זה מטעם ערוה דהא כ' שם הט"ז דכיסוי זכוכית מהני בנשים רוחצות משא"כ בתשמיש המטה בעינן שלא תתראה המזוזה).

10. או"ח סי' ע"ה סעיף א' ברמ"א ובמ"ב ס"ק ח', דמקומות המכוסים אינם נחשבים ערוה לגבי אשה אחרת ובלבד שתהא גופה מכוסה מחציה ולמטה.

11. אבה"ע סי' כ"א; דקול באשה ערוה לגבי איש ואסור אף שלא בשעת תורה ותפלה. ובתולות דידן כולן בחזקת נדות, וכן כ' המשנה ברורה בסי' ע"ה ס"ק י"ז ולכן אסור לשמוע קולן.

א) **ובקול פנויה טהורה אין איסור**, וכן דעת הפמ"ג או"ח במש"ז סוסי' ע"ה והמשנה ברורה שם ס"ק י"ז, ובלבד שלא יכוון ליהנות מקולה שלא יבא לידי הרהור. ובתינוקות קטנות עוד קיל יותר וע' שו"ת איגרות משה או"ח סי' כ"ו משכ"ב.

אבל בשעת תורה ותפילה אסור דלא גרע מקול אשתו.

וקול פנויה עכו"ם ואפילו ילדה קטנה אסור דנחשבת כערוה, עיי"ש במ"ב.

ב) **וקול אשה על ידי רדיו או גרמופון** יש לדון מכח ב' צדדים: (א) אם נחשב הקול כערוה, (ב) דלא גרע מבגדי צבעונים כשיש חשש שיבא לידי הרהור. והאחרונים דנו דאם מכירה ודאי אסור. ואם אינו מכירה יש מצדדים להתיר אפילו ברדיו וכ"ש בגרמופון אבל בשו"ת חלקת יעקב ועוד אחרונים אוסרים בהחלט ברדיו כי שומעים קול ערוה ממש ועצם השמיעה אסורה ולא מטעם חשש הרהור. וכולם

⇐

חוששים שכתעברה אף שפירסה נדה בינתיים כמבואר בפוסקים, וע׳
בשו״ת האחרונים.

CHAPTER 5

צניעות

TZNIUS IN HALOCHO

1.   יש בזה ב׳ איסורים ששניהם מן התורה: א) משום פריצות ב)
מטעם לפני עור שמכשלת את האנשים. והמקור בש״ע אבה״ע סי׳
קט״ו סעיף ד׳ דאשה שטווה בשוק ומגלית זרועותיה יוצאת בלא
כתובה ואף שהוא דרך מלאכתה, וכ״יש שאר חלקי הגוף. ועוד מבואר
באו״ח סי׳ ע״ה דכל חלק גופה שדרכה לכסות נחשב ערוה. ואין
להתחשב עם מה שהדרך בזמננו, כי תלוי על ״מנהג הצניעות שנהגו
בנות ישראל״ כלשון הש״ע הנ״ל, ואחרת הוא מנהג פריצות וזה פשוט
לכל יודע דת ודין, וכן הוא במ״ב סי׳ ע״ה ס״ק ב׳;

ואם מגלית טפח נראה דיש בזה איסור תורה והוא ק״ו מגילוי
שער ראשה שהוא איסור תורה.

ובענין לבישת מכנסיים לנשים ע׳ במנחת יצחק ח״ב סי׳ ק״ח
ובשות׳ אגרות משה יו״ד סי׳ פ״א חומר האיסור מטעם לא תהי׳ כלי
גבר על אשה, חוץ ממה שהוא בעצם מעשה פריצות.

2.   ע״פ משנה ברורה סי׳ ע״ה ס״ק ב׳ אבל החזו״א ועוד הרבה
פוסקים אית להו ״דשוקי״ המוזכר כאן הוא חלק הרגל למטה מן
הארכובה הנקרא (knee) ולא מהני מה שדרכן ללכת כן, ע׳ ב״י ובב״ח
ריש סי׳ ע״ה.

3.   מ״א ריש סי׳ ע״ה.

4.   כנ״ל מספר .1, והאיסור מחמתה. ונראה דאם הבריכה מיוחדת
לנשים אין בו לאסור אף אם לפעמים נכנס לשם איש מפקידי הבריכה,
דהא מקור האיסור משום פריצות וזה לא שייך באופן זה (רק אולי
משום צניעות יש לחוש אבל לא על פי דין). והאיסור שלא להיכנס לשם
הוא על הפקיד אם הוא בן ישראל, אם לא שזה תפקידו מטעמי הצלה.

5.   דאסורים להסתכל במקומות המכוסים שבאשה ועוד משום ולא
תתורו ומגרה יצר הרע, ומשום איסור ונשמרת מכל דבר רע.

לעולם זורה מבחוץ ובא לידי השחתת זרע אסור עמה. מיהו יעשה שאלת חכם. כי יש בזה כמה אופנים שיש היתר.

5. דבמקרה שיש סכנה יש כמה אופנים שיש להתיר ע״פ הגמרא ביבמות דף י״ב, דג׳ נשים משמשות במוך. ואין לעשות בעצמו בלי שאלת רב מובהק.

6. דאסור מן התורה לסרס את האדם בין ישראל בין נכרי, וכן בהמה כמבואר בשו״ע אבה״ע סי׳ ה׳ סעיף י״א וי״ב ובחכ״א כלל קכ״ד סעיף ה׳. ואפילו לאכול איזה סם שעי״ז יסתרס אסור ואפילו במקום רפואה. וכל זה באיש אבל אשה מותרת לאכול סם לסרסה. אבל כשהיא נשואה הרי היא משועבדת לבעלה לפריה ורביה. מיהו אם יש לה צער לידה וכדומה בזה ישתנה הדין עיי״ש בפ״ת סי״ק י״א. ואם סירוס זמני מותר לאיש לצורך רפואה או לצורך פרו ולבו דנו בזה האחרונים ויעשה שאלת חכם.

ובאשה אם עושים מעשה בידים לסרסה ג״כ אסור ולכן בהסרת הרחם ע״י ניתוח יש בזה שאלה של סירוס, ויעשה שאלת חכם. וע״י נכרי במקום חולי קיל כי אמירה לנכרי במקום חולי מותר, וע׳ באחרונים.

וכן בכל מיני טיפולים רפואיים וניתוחים באברי הזרע בין באיש בין באשה ואפילו נעשה לשם רפואה יעשה שאלת חכם. **ובעניין אסור סירוס של נכרי** עי״י ישראל ע׳ בשו״ת מנחת יצחק חי״ה סי׳ י״ב; ובעניין סירוס זמני ע׳ במנח״י חי״ה סי׳ י״ב.

7. לגרום הפלת העובר הוא יותר חמור מהשחתת זרע כי יש לעובר כבר קצת חיות, ונכרי חייב מיתה על כגון זה (אחר מ׳ יום מסירת הולד) ואין חילוק אם עושים זה בידים או ע״י סם, וע׳ בשו״ת האחרונים מה שדנו בזה. וע׳ סנהדרין דף נ״ז ע״ב דבן נח נהרג על הפלת עובר. וע׳ תוס׳ שם נ״ט ד״ה ליכא.

ואפילו אם לדעת הרופאים יש צורך גדול מטעמי בריאות, יש להתישב הרבה אם יש באמת חשש סכנת נפשות, ולא יעשה ח״ו שום מעשה בלי שאלת רב מובהק. ובפרט בזמננו אשר זה כהיתר בעיני הרופאים ולכן אין להאמינים בדרך כלל. ולכן ישאלו גם לרופא ירא שמים.

ועי׳ במשנה אהלות פ״ז מ״ו דאם יש סכנה לאשה מותר להרוג העובר, דהעובר נחשב כרודף המסתכן חייה, ועי״ש בהגה׳ רע״א. ועיין בחו״מ סי׳ תכ״ה סעיף ב׳ (וקודם מ׳ יום אולי קל קצת יותר במקום חשש סכנה, מיהו צריכין לידע בברור שנתעברו קודם מ׳ יום, כי אנו

בשם גדול אחד שאינו ראוי לעשות כן. וידוע שבלי קירוב בשר נתמעט התאוה וזה גורם לאיזה אנשים שאינם באים לידי קישוי גמור וזה גורם לכמה קלקולים. ואין להרבות בדבר שהוא פשוט בגמרא לחיוב. וכן שמעתי בשם גדולים. וקשה לסמוך על מחילתה בזמן הזה.

ומה שכ' בשי"ע או"ח סי' ר"מ סעי' ח' שיש למעט בהנאתו עי"יש ושבעל נפש צריך ליזהר בזה, צ"ל דמיירי במחילתה הגמורה וגם שהוא בעל נפש. אך מ"מ נראה מן המ"ב שם דמסכים שראוי לשמש ערום.

25. דממה שאמרו שצריכים קירוב בשר אנחנו למדים דאינו יוצא חיוב עונה אא"כ נותן לה כל הנאתה ולכל מה שהיא תואות. ובכלל זה לשהות אצלה קצת זמן גם אחר התשמיש.

26. שי"ע או"ח סי' ר"מ סעי' י"ד.

27. ולכן אין ראוי לאחר זמן העונה כי יש בזה גרם של גזילה אם יהיה חלש ועיף ביום מחר. ואף שענין גדול הוא שהזמן יהיה אחר חצות לילה, מ"מ במקום שיש חשש חטא אין להביט על ענינים שאין מקורם בש"ס. וזה חוץ ממה שכבר כתבתי בציון 16 שיש גם להתחשב עמה. וכהיום שלפי שעון הקיץ החצות נתאחר עד אחר שעה אחד דומה שלרוב נשים ובני אדם קשה לקיים את זה, וע' במ"ב שם ס"ק לי"ד.

CHAPTER 3

מניעת הריון

THE TORAH VIEW ON FAMILY PLANNING

1. אבן העזר סי' א' סעי' א' וח'.

2. שם סעי' ג'.

3. שם סעי' ד'. גם אמרו יטע כרם ואח"כ ישא אשה.

4. והטעם משום אסור השחתת זרע אשר הוא בעצם חטא שיש בו עונש מיתה בידי שמים. ואף שלא מצינו עונש מיתה באופן כזה, מכל מקום הוא מן החמורות שבחמורות. וכן אף האשה אסורה לעשות שום פעולה להימנע ההריון בין לפני תשמיש בין לאחר תשמיש. והבעל מותר באשתו רק באופן שתהא ראויה להתעבר. ואף שמותר לבא על זקנה או אשה שאינה בת בנים היינו משום דהוא בא עליה כדרך כל הארץ. ולכן מותר אף אם הרופאים הסירו רחמה על ידי ניתוח. אבל אשה שיש לה אוטם ברחם מבואר בשי"ע אבעי"ה סי' כ"ג סעיף ה' שאם

⇐

14. או"ח סי' רי"מ סעי' א' ומ"ב סי"ק יי"ב וע"י אבה"ע סי' כ"ה
סעי' ב'.

15. כמו שהאיש משועבד לאשתו כן היא משועבדת לו. ואף דעבודתו
היא למעט בהנאה מ"מ היא מצדה חייבת לעשות את שלה כהוגן.

16. דטעם חיוב עונה הוא כדי שהבעל יְהַנֶה את אשתו ואם היא עייפה
אינה נהנית כל צרכה ועוד שיש צד עינוי כשמשתנת עליו והוא מאחר
לבוא וגם בזה שייך זריזים מקדימים למצוה כשמכוון לשם שמים
שלא לַעֲנוֹתָה.

17. ראה ציון 16

18. או"ח סי' רי"מ סעי' א'

19. רמב"ם פ"ה הל' דעות הל' ה'.

20. שם סעי' י'.

21. שם סעי' ט'.

22. כעין מה שהזהירה נעמי את רות בקשר לבועז: ורחצת וסכת
ושמת שמלתיך עליך. ואמרו אשה מקושטת לתי"ח (שבת כ"ה.).

23. והשל"ה הקדוש כותב בשער האותיות אות דרך ארץ וז"ל:
מתקשטת תמיד לפניו בענוה ובחן ובצניעות ויהיו בגדיה בכל עת
נקיים.

24. הובא בסידור ר' יעקב עמדין בהנהגת ליל שבת בחוליא ג',ג'
ומיוסד על מה שאמרו בגמרא האומר אי אפשי אלא הוא בבגדו והיא
בבגדה יוציא ויתן כתובה כתובות מ"ח. ונפסק בש"ע אבה"ע סי' ע"ו
סעי' י"ג דמדאורייתא בעינן בשר קירוב בשר דווקא. עי' המשך במילואים.

ומה שאמרו שהקב"ה שונא למי שמשמש ערום היינו שצריך
לכסות עצמו למעלה בסדין או במצע, ומסיים שבודאי צריכים פישוט
בגדים אף שאינו מעכב כשיש איזה סיבה המונעת, וכי"ש היכא שמחלה
והובא גם בשער הציון של המי"ב בסי' רי"מ סי"ק יי"ח בשם המקובלים.

ומלשון הגמרא משמע דזהו זכותה והוה בכלל שארה ועונתה לא
יגרע. (ואם אינה דורשת את זה בתחילת הנישואין היינו משום דלא
טעמה עדיין טעם ביאה.) אך ברמ"א באה"ע סי' ע"ו סעי' ג' ע"י כתב דכן
בהפך דאם היא אומרת כן שתשמש רק בבגדה תצא בלא כתובה.

ועי' שם בחלקת מחוקק דאם אינו עושה כן (לשמש ערום) נחשב
כאילו לא קיים עונה כלל ונחשב מורד. ופלא עצום על מה שנתפרסם

⇐

שאינו חם בטבעו או מי שנתרגל באשתו כל כך עד שאין המגע הזמני
מעורר את תאותו, אצלו ודאי מותר וגם מצוה לפעמים לשמח את
אשתו. וכן שמעתי מגדולי הפוסקים ויש הוכחות לזה מן השי"ע.
ואחרים אשר אינם בבחינה זו יעשו שאלת חכם. ומי שמרגיש בעצמו
שההנהגה הקרובה לאשתו מזקת לרוחניות שלו (דהרי זהו בגדר אין
לדבר סוף) אדם כזה אינו מחויב להקריב את עצמו ואת רוחניותו
ותורתו כדי לעשות נחת רוח לאשתו באמצע היום, ועליו למצוא עצות
אחרות כדי להעמידה על סיפוקה (על ידי שיחה או שאר סימני אהבה
ויתכן שחובתו להוסיף על זמני העונה שלה כי יש נשים הצריכות את
זה יותר משאר נשים).

2.   כמו שאמרו חז"ל: לא ניתנו מצוות לישראל אלא לצרף בהם את
      הבריות (ויקרא רבא י"ג, ג').

3.   עי' לשון הרמב"ם הל' דעות פ"ה הל' ד' ומסיים ויבעול בבושה
      ולא בעזות ולשון השי"ע אבה"ע סי' כ"ה סעי' ב' וז"ל צנוע מאד
      בשעת תשמיש.

      ואברהם אבינו היה כל כך צנוע דלא ידע ביופי של שרה שלא
      נסתכל בה ורק כשבא למצרים נתודע לו (ע' ב"ב ט"ז.).

4.   או"ח סי' ר"מ סעי' י"א.

5.   שם ובאבה"ע סי' כ"ה סעי' ה' דנחשב דרך עזות פנים. ואף דבבית
      אפל משמע דמותר על פי דין כמבואר שם באו"ח, מ"מ אין דרך בני
      ישראל לשמש ביום. (אך עי' ביצה ז'.) וכשיצרו מתגבר עליו מתיר
      החכ"א עי' בשער ציון של המ"ב ס"ק כ"ח.

6.   סי' ר"מ סעי' ו' ובמ"ב שם.

7.   אבה"ע סי' כ"ה סעי' ד'.

8.   או"ח סי' ד' סעי' י"ח. עי"פ דין די בפעם אחת ויש מחמירים
      לרחוץ ג' פעמים מ"ב שם ס"ק ל"ט.

9.   או"ח סי' ר"מ סעי' ט'.

10.   שם סעי' י'.

11.   שם במ"ב ס"ק נ"ד. ואף שכ' באשה נראה דלא דבר אלא בהוה
      והוא הדין להפך ופשוט.

12.   שם סעי' ו' וז'. ולענין תינוק מביא המ"ב בס"ק נ"ד בשם הזוהר
      להחמיר.

13.   שם סעי' א'.

⇐

בגרי"א. וא"כ בוודאי לא תקנו חז"ל שחייבת לעבוד חוץ לביתה, ובפרט שיש בזה לפעמים כמה פקפוקים. אך מאידך גיסא יש מקום לומר דכהיום שבלא"ה דרך הנשים לילך לחוץ אולי נשתנה הדין וצע"ג.

11. דהרי גם ללמוד האומנות צריכה לצאת מביתה.

12. דהכל בכלל תקנת חז"ל.

13. דיני נכסי אשתו מיוסדים על אבה"ע סי' פ"ח סעי' א'-ב', סעי' ז', סעי' י"א וסעי' י"ז. ומה שכתבתי בסוף שיעשה שאלת חכם היינו משום שאסור למכור נכסי מלוג של אשתו.

14. עי' ברכות סוף כ"ז: בר' אליעזר שאמר איזיל ואימליך באשתי. ואמרו (ב"מ נ"ט.) שישמע לעצת אשתו לחד לשון במילי דביתא ולחד לשון אף במילי דעלמא אבל לא במילי דשמיא.

15. יו"ד סי' ר"מ סעי' י"ז, וז"ל שאשה משועבדת לבעלה לפיכך היא פטורה מכבוד אב ואם. וכי' הש"ך דאם אין הבעל מקפיד חייבת בכל דבר כמו האיש.

CHAPTER 2

CONDUCT OF TZNIUS FOR HUSBAND AND WIFE

1. הזמן המסוגל לזה ביותר הוא בזמן העונה. ובענין חיבוק ונישוק בשאר זמנים בעצם מוכח מן הפוסקים דמותר דרק בסמוך לווסתה (כלומר ביום שיש לחוש שיבא) אשר חייב לפרוש מאשתו על פי דין יש דיון בפוסקים אם מותר בחיבוק ונישוק (עי' יו"ד סי' קפ"ד סעי' ב' ובש"ך וט"ז ובפ"ת שם) אבל בשאר זמנים מותר, אך בתנאי שלא יבא ח"ו לידי הוצאת זרע. ויש רק לדון האם יש לחוש שיבא לידי קישוי. והנה בספר טהרת ישראל בבאר יצחק ס"ק כ"א דן בדעת הפוסקים המתירים חו"נ סמוך לווסתה וכותב מדעתו דמיירי דווקא באיש שאינו מחומם כל כך אשר בטוח שלא יבא לידי קישוי אבר וגם לא לידי הוז"ל ומוסיף דאף כשהיא טהורה ג"כ אין חו"נ מותר אלא בשברור לו שלא יבא לידי קישוי. והנה באופן שהיא טהורה יש לדון להתיר שהרי יש לו פת בסלו. אך בעיקר נראה דתלוי על טבע האדם כי יש אנשים חמים בטבעם אשר החיבור של חיבוק ונישוק מחמם אותם ובאים לידי קישוי והוצאת זרע וזה וודאי אסור. ולפעמים יבא לידי טומאה בלילה אם לא באופן שבדעתו לבעול באותה לילה. אך מי

CHAPTER 1

MARRIAGE OBLIGATIONS

1. אבה"ע סי' סי"ט יי"ז: כשנושא אדם אשה מתחייב לה בעשרה דברים,מזונותיה , כסותה, ועונתה, ועיקר כתובתה (אם ימות או יגרשנה), רפואתה, חיוב לפדותה, קבורתה, ועוד כמה חיובי כתובה עיי"ש.והפרטים מבוארים בכמה סימנים שם.

2. שם סי' עי"ז סעי' ב' בענין עונה ובסי' פ' לענין מעשה ידיה ומלאכה.

3. אבן העזר סי' ע' סעי' א' לענין מזונות, וסי' ע"ג לענין כסות, ולענין רפואה בסי' ע"ט והשל"ה כתב "צרכי הנשים מרובים ויש דברים הכרחיים לשמירת גופה ולענין ההולדה וההנקה".

4. עיי"ש הפרטים בשי"ע ובחלקת מחוקק סי"ק א'.

5. עי' בסי' ע"א בחלקת מחוקק סי"ק א'. ולרמב"ם דס"ל דמזונות אשתו מן התורה פשוט שהיא קודמת ע' בבית שמואל סי' סי"ט סי"ק א'.

6. עי' סי' ע' בחלקת מחוקק א' דמהנה מחילה.

7. סי' ע"א בחלקת מחוקק סי"ק מ"ג וע' יותר פרטים בסי' פ' סעי' ד' וז"ל רוחצת לבעלה פניו ידיו ורגליו (אך לא נוהגים כן כי הוא מוחל) ומוזגת לו את הכוס (כלומר מושטת המאכלים) ומצעת לו המטה (ויי"א דמחוייבת להציע כל מטות הבית) ועומדת ומשמשת בפני בעלה כגון שנתן לו מים או כלי או שתטול מלפניו וכיוצא בדברים אלו. ועיי"ש עוד בסעי' ו'.

8. סי' פ' סעי' א'.

9. עי' בבאר היטב שם סי"ק א' ובפ"ת שם סי"ק א' ובדגול מרבבה. אך אין הדבר מוחלט ולכן ראוי ליתן לה מה שרוצית בהרחבה, דיכולה היא לומר קים לי כדעת הפוסקים שאם זן אותה מעשה ידיה שלה.

10. דחיוב מלאכה מדינא דגמרא רק בדברים שעושה בביתה כמו טוית צמר או פשתים. אבל לענין לילך לחוץ הרי כל כבודה בת מלך פנימה. וע" בסי' ע"ג סעי' א' ברמ"א שכתב שאשה לא תרגיל עצמה לצאת הרבה "שאין יופי לאשה אלא לישב בזוית ביתה" ועיי"ש

⇐